The Internet and Crime

D1298378

POINT
COUNTERPOINT

The Internet and Crime

By Alan Marzilli, M.A., J.D.

SERIES EDITOR
Alan Marzilli, M.A., J.D.

CHELSEA HOUSE
PUBLISHERS
An imprint of Infobase Publishing

The Internet and Crime

4/12/10
Uby
$ 35 —

Chelsea House
An imprint of Infobase Publishing
132 West 31st Street
New York, NY 10001

Library of Congress Cataloging-in-Publication Data
Marzilli, Alan.
   The Internet and crime / By Alan Marzilli.
       p. cm.
   Includes bibliographical references and index.
   ISBN 978-1-60413-506-0 (hardcover)
   1. Internet—Law and legislation—United States—Criminal provisions.
   2. Computer crimes—United States. 3. Internet fraud—United States.
   4. Consumer protection—Law and legislation—United States. I. Title.

   KF390.5.C6M375 2009
   345.73'0268—dc22

                               2009022139

Chelsea House books are available at special discounts when purchased in bulk quantities for businesses, associations, institutions, or sales promotions. Please call our Special Sales Department in New York at (212) 967-8800 or (800) 322-8755.

You can find Chelsea House on the World Wide Web at http://www.chelseahouse.com.

Text design by Keith Trego
Cover design by Takeshi Takahashi
Composition by EJB Publishing Services
Cover printed by Bang Printing, Brainerd, MN
Book printed and bound by Bang Printing, Brainerd, MN
Date printed: November, 2009

Printed in the United States of America

10 9 8 7 6 5 4 3 2 1

This book is printed on acid-free paper.

All links and Web addresses were checked and verified to be correct at the time of publication. Because of the dynamic nature of the Web, some addresses and links may have changed since publication and may no longer be valid.

POINT ||||

◁||||| COUNTERPOINT

FOREWORD |||||▷

Alan Marzilli, M.A., J.D.
Birmingham, Alabama

The POINT/COUNTERPOINT series offers the reader a greater under-standing of some of the most controversial issues in contemporary American society—issues such as capital punishment, immigration, gay rights, and gun control. We have looked for the most contem-porary issues and have included topics—such as the controversies surrounding "blogging"—that we could not have imagined when the series began.

In each volume, the author has selected an issue of particular importance and set out some of the key arguments on both sides of the issue. Why study both sides of the debate? Maybe you have yet to make up your mind on an issue, and the arguments presented in the book will help you to form an opinion. More likely, however, you will already have an opinion on many of the issues covered by the series. There is always the chance that you will change your opinion after reading the arguments for the other side. But even if you are firmly committed to an issue—for example, school prayer or animal rights—reading both sides of the argument will help you to become a more effective advo-cate for your cause. By gaining an understanding of opposing argu-ments, you can develop answers to those arguments.

Perhaps more importantly, listening to the other side sometimes helps you see your opponent's arguments in a more human way. For example, Sister Helen Prejean, one of the nation's most visible oppo-nents of capital punishment, has been deeply affected by her interac-tions with the families of murder victims. By seeing the families' grief and pain, she understands much better why people support the death penalty, and she is able to carry out her advocacy with a greater sensi-tivity to the needs and beliefs of death penalty supporters.

The books in the series include numerous features that help the reader to gain a greater understanding of the issues. Real-life examples illustrate the human side of the issues. Each chapter also includes excerpts from relevant laws, court cases, and other material, which provide a better foundation for understanding the arguments. The volumes contain citations to relevant sources of law and information, and an appendix guides the reader through the basics of legal research, both on the Internet and in the library. Today, through free Web sites, it is easy to access legal documents, and these books might give you ideas for your own research.

Studying the issues covered by the POINT/COUNTERPOINT series is more than an academic activity. The issues described in the books affect all of us as citizens. They are the issues that today's leaders debate and tomorrow's leaders will decide. While all of the issues covered in the POINT/COUNTERPOINT series are controversial today, and will remain so for the foreseeable future, it is entirely possible that the reader might one day play a central role in resolving the debate. Today it might seem that some debates—such as capital punishment and abortion—will never be resolved.

However, our nation's history is full of debates that seemed as though they never would be resolved, and many of the issues are now well settled—at least on the surface. In the nineteenth century, abolitionists met with widespread resistance to their efforts to end slavery. Ultimately, the controversy threatened the union, leading to the Civil War between the northern and southern states. Today, while a public debate over the merits of slavery would be unthinkable, racism persists in many aspects of society.

Similarly, today nobody questions women's right to vote. Yet at the beginning of the twentieth century, suffragists fought public battles for women's voting rights, and it was not until the passage of the Nineteenth Amendment in 1920 that the legal right of women to vote was established nationwide.

What makes an issue controversial? Often, controversies arise when most people agree that there is a problem but disagree about the best way to solve it. There is little argument that poverty is a major problem in the United States, especially in inner cities and rural areas. Yet, people disagree vehemently about the best way to address the problem. To some, the answer is social programs, such as welfare, food stamps, and public housing. However, many argue that such subsidies encourage dependence on government benefits while unfairly penalizing those who work and pay taxes, and that the real solution is to require people to support themselves.

American society is in a constant state of change, and sometimes modern practices clash with what many consider to be "traditional values," which are often rooted in conservative political views or religious beliefs. Many blame high crime rates, and problems such as poverty, illiteracy, and drug use on the breakdown of the traditional family structure of a married mother and father raising their children. Since the "sexual revolution" of the 1960s and 1970s, sparked in part by the widespread availability of the birth control pill, marriage rates have declined, and the number of children born outside of marriage has increased. The sexual revolution led to controversies over birth control, sex education, and other issues, most prominently abortion. Similarly, the gay rights movement has been challenged as a threat to traditional values. While many gay men and lesbians want to have the same right to marry and raise families as heterosexuals, many politicians and others have challenged gay marriage and adoption as a threat to American society.

Sometimes, new technology raises issues that we have never faced before, and society disagrees about the best solution. Are people free to swap music online, or does this violate the copyright laws that protect songwriters and musicians' ownership of the music that they create? Should scientists use "genetic engineering" to create new crops that are resistant to disease and pests and produce more food, or is it too risky to use a laboratory to create plants that nature never intended? Modern medicine has continued to increase the average lifespan—which is now 77 years, up from under 50 years at the beginning of the twentieth century—but many people are now choosing to die in comfort rather than living with painful ailments in their later years. For doctors, this presents an ethical dilemma: should they allow their patients to die? Should they assist patients in ending their own lives painlessly?

Perhaps the most controversial issues are those that implicate a Constitutional right. The Bill of Rights—the first 10 Amendments to the U.S. Constitution—spells out some of the most fundamental rights that distinguish our democracy from other nations with fewer freedoms. However, the sparsely worded document is open to interpretation, with each side saying that the Constitution is on their side. The Bill of Rights was meant to protect individual liberties; however, the needs of some individuals clash with society's needs. Thus, the Constitution often serves as a battleground between individuals and government officials seeking to protect society in some way. The First Amendment's guarantee of "freedom of speech" leads to some very difficult questions. Some forms of expression—such as burning an American flag—lead to public outrage, but are protected by the First Amendment. Other types of expression that most people find objectionable—such as child pornography—are not protected by the Constitution. The question is not only where to draw the line, but whether drawing lines around constitutional rights threatens our liberty.

The Bill of Rights raises many other questions about individual rights and societal "good." Is a prayer before a high school football game an "establishment of religion" prohibited by the First Amendment? Does the Second Amendment's promise of "the right to bear arms" include concealed handguns? Does stopping and frisking someone standing on a known drug corner constitute "unreasonable search and seizure" in violation of the Fourth Amendment? Although the U.S. Supreme Court has the ultimate authority in interpreting the U.S. Constitution, its answers do not always satisfy the public. When a group of nine people—sometimes by a five-to-four vote—makes a decision that affects hundreds of millions of others, public outcry can be expected. For example, the Supreme Court's 1973 ruling in *Roe v. Wade* that abortion is protected by the Constitution did little to quell the debate over abortion.

Whatever the root of the controversy, the books in the POINT/ COUNTERPOINT series seek to explain to the reader the origins of the debate, the current state of the law, and the arguments on either side of the debate. Our hope in creating this series is that readers will be better informed about the issues facing not only our politicians, but all of our nation's citizens, and become more actively involved in resolving these debates, as voters, concerned citizens, journalists, or maybe even elected officials.

Much has happened in the years since the POINT/COUNTERPOINT series first examined controversies over regulating the Internet. Some problems have been solved with new laws or new technologies. In many cases both legislation and technology were used to fix these problems, yet it is debatable, for example, whether a federal law blocking spam has done more to reduce unwanted e-mails than new software.

As new technologies have made the Web more interactive, people have found new ways to exploit this aspect of the Web. Online marketplaces like eBay and Craigslist make it easier to sell and buy merchandise, but this ease extends to stolen merchandise, angering many "brick and mortar" retailers. As teens and young adults use Facebook and other social networking sites to express themselves and meet others, sexual predators use the sites to look for victims. While online pharmacies might create convenience and cost savings, drug enforcement officials have fought to keep drugs of abuse from being sold without oversight. Because almost any restriction of the Internet to protect the public necessarily restricts some valid use, efforts to combat Internet crime often meet with strong protests from civil libertarians, entrepreneurs, and others who want to keep the Internet a "wild frontier."

Safe Surfing

Dear Reader,

I am a prominent Nigerian businessman. Unfortunately, a bank account of mine containing several million dollars (U.S.) has been tied up in a political dispute. My attorney has advised me that one way of clearing up this dispute will be to transfer the money into a U.S. bank account held by a U.S. citizen. At that point, the Nigerian government will no longer be able to restrict use of my funds. I am humbly requesting your assistance. If you will permit me to transfer my funds into your account, I will allow you to keep 2 percent of the money. This amounts to approximately $45,000 U.S. However, in order to pay my attorney, I am in great need of an advance sum of $2,200 U.S. I will need you to transfer this money directly into my attorney's account before he will set up the transfer of my funds into your account. If you are interested in my offer, *please respond to my e-mail with your full name, date of birth, Social Security Number, bank name, and account number.*

Sounds too good to be true? It is. You may be surprised, however, how many people have fallen for such schemes over the years. For a while, these Nigerian "pay in advance" schemes were so rampant that the U.S. Secret Service had to devote an investigation unit to "419 schemes," named after a section of the Nigerian criminal code that outlaws them. According to the U.S. government's OnGuard Online Web site:

> The emails are from crooks trying to steal your money or your identity. Inevitably, in this scenario, emergencies come up, requiring more of your money and delaying the "transfer" of funds to your account. In the end, there aren't any profits for you, and the scam artist vanishes with your money. The harm sometimes can be felt even beyond your pocketbook: according to State Department reports, people who have responded to "pay in advance" solicitations have been beaten, subjected to threats and extortion, and in some cases, murdered.[1]

Unfortunately, the Nigerian e-mail scheme is only one of hundreds of ways that criminals have learned to take advantage of the low cost and convenience of the Internet. Rather than going through the cost and risk of seeking out victims in person, by phone, or by letter, criminals can search for information quickly and inexpensively, and send out millions of messages to would-be victims.

The Development of the Internet into a High-Crime Zone

The Internet originated in 1969 with the linking of computers at several distant university research laboratories. The U.S. government sponsored the development and expansion of this computer network, known as ARPANET (Advanced Research Projects Agency Network), as it was seen as a way of keeping the United States technologically ahead of the Soviet Union and its allies. For years, the network allowed scientists and engineers to communicate information, but it remained the domain of "techies." The average person might have known about the existence of the computer network from watching movies such as 1983's *War Games*, in which a young Matthew Broderick played a teen who inadvertently hacked into a military network and could have started a nuclear war. Only a tiny percentage of the population, however, had the technical expertise to communicate over computer networks—not to mention the hardware. At the time, computers generally needed to connect directly to another computer.

As online communications became more popular during the 1980s, computer networks sought to improve both the utility of their services by making connections easier and the usability of their services by making the interface less intimidating. Eventually, commercial services such as CompuServe and America Online began offering consumers a way to connect with other users much more easily, with a user interface that included graphics and simple "keywords" rather than strings of code. These advances brought millions of users online starting in the mid-1990s. Making it much easier for people who lacked technical expertise to get online, however, had an unintended consequence. Suddenly millions of naïve users became easy targets for criminals and unscrupulous businesspeople. Scams such as the "advance pay" e-mails from Nigeria proliferated, as did unwanted e-mail, which came to be known as "spam."

Additionally, as it became easier to share photographs and videos, pornography flourished. Because child pornography is illegal, its purveyors found ways to share it while maintaining their anonymity. As it became possible to easily create and share music files, record labels balked at users sharing their music collections through online services such as Napster.

Legislative and Judicial Solutions

The first significant reaction of Congress and the state legislatures to widespread consumer use of the Internet was with regard to the politically charged issue of pornography. Congress passed a series of laws, including the Communications Decency Act of 1996, which banned making "obscene" or "indecent" material available on the Internet. Under the law, "indecent" material that could be shown in R-rated movies in theaters would have been illegal on the Internet. (For material to be considered "obscene," it had to meet a strict legal test that showed it had no redeeming qualities whatsoever.) The courts wasted no time in declaring the section of the law relating to "indecent" material unconstitutional under the First Amendment's guarantee of free speech, and the U.S. Supreme Court upheld this decision in the case *Reno v. ACLU*.[2]

Unable to regulate the content of the Internet, Congress sought to protect children from explicit content by prohibiting access to such sites by people younger than 18. The Child Online Protection Act (COPA)[3] required operators of commercial pornography sites to deny access to minors; however, the U.S. Supreme Court ruled the law was also unconstitutional in *Ashcroft v. ACLU*.[4] The ensuing Children's Internet Protection Act (CIPA) was upheld by the Supreme Court.[5] CIPA requires that schools and libraries that receive federal funding for telecommunications must install "filtering" software to prevent minors from accessing material that is "harmful to minors."[6]

When it came to file sharing on services such as Napster and Grokster, the issue was "intellectual property," or the idea that the creators of music, movies, artwork, etc., have the right to control how their creations are distributed, including the right to charge money for them. While Congress held hearings on file-swapping, ultimately it could not agree on an amendment to the federal copyright law that specifically addressed the topic. (Coincidentally, in 1998, Congress had passed the ambitiously named Digital Millennium Copyright Act,[7] a complex law that addressed making recordings on VHS tapes, but Congress had been unable to predict the quandary caused by file-swapping.)

Although Congress failed to act on file-swapping, the U.S. Supreme Court, in a 2005 case, ruled that the owners of intellectual property could sue the makers of software such as

FROM THE BENCH

United States v. American Library Association, 539 U.S. 194 (2003)

Librarians challenged a federal law that required libraries to install Internet filtering software on publicly accessible computers in order to qualify for federal telecommunications funding. The Supreme Court rejected their argument that it placed libraries in the position of censoring speech:

> A public library does not acquire Internet terminals in order to create a public forum for Web publishers to express themselves, any more than it collects books in order to provide a public forum for the authors of books to speak. It provides Internet access, not to "encourage a diversity of views from private speakers," ... but for the same reasons it offers other library resources: to facilitate research, learning, and recreational pursuits by furnishing materials of requisite and appropriate quality....
>
> A library's need to exercise judgment in making collection decisions depends on its traditional role in identifying suitable and worthwhile material; it is no less entitled to play that role when it collects material from the Internet than when it collects material from any other source. Most libraries already exclude pornography from their print collections because they deem it inappropriate for inclusion. We do not subject these decisions to heightened scrutiny; it would make little sense to treat libraries' judgments to block online pornography any differently, when these judgments are made for just the same reason.
>
> Moreover, because of the vast quantity of material on the Internet and the rapid pace at which it changes, libraries cannot possibly segregate, item by item, all the Internet material that is appropriate for inclusion from all that is not. While a library could limit its Internet collection to just those sites it found worthwhile, it could do so only at the cost of excluding an enormous amount of valuable information that it lacks the capacity to review. Given that tradeoff, it is entirely reasonable for public libraries to reject that approach and instead exclude certain categories of content, without making individualized judgments that everything they do make available has requisite and appropriate quality.

Grokster and StreamCast, which allowed users to trade and share copyrighted music under existing copyright law. The Court held: "One who distributes a device with the object of promoting its use to infringe copyright, as shown by clear expression or other affirmative steps taken to foster infringement, is liable for the resulting acts of infringement by third parties."[8]

Perhaps seeking the approval of constituents frustrated with constant e-mails advertising herbal remedies, pornography, and thousands of other unwanted goods and services, Congress passed a law regulating spam in 2003. Many, however, thought the so-called "CAN-SPAM Act"[9] was too weak. In the long run, it is difficult to tell how effective the law has been, because e-mail providers have used increasingly sophisticated software to keep spam from clogging their users' inboxes.

Ongoing Problems

As problems go away or are successfully legislated or litigated, new ones pop up. One of the biggest Internet-related crimes is identity theft, or stealing personal information in order to raid bank accounts or borrow money in another person's name. Identity thieves often use the technique of "phishing," or drawing an unsuspecting user to a bogus Web site that asks for personal information. For example, they might send an e-mail notifying the recipient that he or she must change the PIN for his or her ATM card. Of course, the Web link provided is to a site that looks just like the bank's, and the person who enters a bank account number and corresponding PIN will soon have his or her account drained by the thieves.

Crimes such as identity theft are significant, but they are not really controversial. Other than the thieves themselves, nobody really supports identity theft, and this is one area where banks, consumers, and politicians might actually be in agreement. On the other hand, cracking down on other types of crime requires infringing on the rights of legitimate online activity and thus generates controversy. Take, for example, the use of popular sites for buying and selling items, such as eBay, Amazon.com's Market-place, and Craigslist. On these sites, the operator of the site is not the one actually in possession of the merchandise. Thus, there is no way for the site to guarantee that the merchandise is not stolen. Some, particularly retailers hit hard by shoplifters, have called on these "online marketplaces" to restrict sales in certain ways that discourage the sale of stolen merchandise. Placing restrictions on sales, however, ultimately leads to increased costs, both to sellers and buyers.

Another controversial topic is the sale of prescription drugs over the Internet. Some doctors and consumer activists have fought to allow doctors to write prescriptions to people who visit a site and provide health information. They say it reduces health care costs, particularly for people without insurance and rural Americans, who do not have easy access to doctors. Doctors' groups, however, adamantly oppose the practice because it puts people at risk to get prescription drugs outside of the traditional doctor-patient relationship. Many are concerned that these sites even encourage drug abuse.

An issue that took legislators (and many other adults) by surprise was the sudden proliferation of social-networking sites like MySpace and Facebook. Although these sites have their own policies for access by minors, some in Congress are concerned that the sites are hunting grounds for sexual predators, and they would like to ban these sites from allowing minors without their parents' permission and oversight. Critics of these laws say they are unworkable and ignore the value of these sites, not to mention teens' resiliency and ability to protect themselves with a little education and support.

Summary

Once a technologically challenging puzzle, the Internet has become a user-friendly entertainment venue, shopping mall, and town square. As an ever-increasing percentage of the population gets online, however, criminals are seizing the opportunity to seek out new victims. Sales of stolen property and illegal drugs, and solicitation of minors by sexual predators are just a few of the issues facing Internet users today. Not everyone agrees, however, on the best way to address these issues, because many want the Internet to remain largely unregulated.

Regulation of Online Auction and Classified Sites Will Hurt Commerce

Coin dealer Troy Thoreson is lucky—he is able to make a profit by doing something he loves. To be successful, however, he has to market his products well beyond his hometown of Los Banos, California. Before 1998, he mostly sold coins and other collectibles at coin shows and by mail order. That year, however, his business took off when he started selling his merchandise on eBay.

The popular online auction site, eBay, has made life much easier for collectors of all types. In fact, the site was created as a way for collectors to buy and sell Pez candy dispensers. From the convenience of their home computers, coin collectors nation-wide can log onto eBay and search the inventory offered by Thoreson's store and thousands of other coin dealers, then place bids on the coins they are looking for. The Web site acts as an auctioneer, with different collectors placing increasing bids until the auction closes and the highest bidder gets the item.

Auction sites like eBay do not sell anything themselves. Instead, they offer a forum for buyers and sellers to connect, generally charging a set fee to list an item for sale, a percentage from each sale, or both. Said Thoreson:

> It's a great venue for those looking to make it big on the Internet. A lot of people do not realize the cost involved in the development of a Web site. Many will find they are disappointed once they realize how difficult and expensive it can be to drive traffic to your own site. With eBay Stores, it doesn't cost a lot to make your own Store a reality.[1]

Other sites operate more like traditional newspaper classified ads. The most popular of these sites, Craigslist, started as a free service; as of this writing it charges nothing for most ads. In a few cities, Craigslist charges for help-wanted ads, and in New York City, the site charges for some real estate ads. With more than 40 million users in the United States and millions more internationally, Craigslist has retained its barebones appearance and a small staff of about 25 people in order to continue offering free listings. Without the sophisticated bidding and shipping tools of eBay, merchandise sold on Craigslist is typically sold (or given away) locally. Anyone can list items for sale on Craigslist, making it much more efficient than the traditional yard sale or flea market. Sellers often get dozens of responses, some from users who have saved searches that are automatically updated, thus alerting them whenever an item they want is offered for sale.

While eBay and Craigslist have been the most successful auction and classified sites, respectively, many other sites offer similar services to buyers and sellers. Amazon.com, for example, acts both as a "traditional" merchant selling its own merchandise and offering third parties the opportunity to create "stores" to sell new and used merchandise through the Amazon.com site. Someone who searches for a particular book on Amazon.com buys it new directly from Amazon.com or might also have the opportunity to purchase it used from someone operating a "store" on the site.

While these sites have many happy buyers and sellers, some people are concerned that there is not enough oversight of auction and classified sites. Because the operators of the sites never have physical control over merchandise that is offered for sale, sellers may act dishonestly, such as by offering stolen or counterfeit merchandise or by simply taking money and not delivering the product. The operators of the sites have taken various steps to prevent this dishonesty, and they, along with millions of happy users, do not want to see the government bog down the flow of "e-commerce" with unnecessary laws.

Sites such as eBay and Craigslist reduce transaction costs to consumers' benefit.

Legitimate online transactions (i.e., transactions not involving stolen or counterfeit merchandise) have many benefits for both buyers and sellers. Before eBay and Craigslist, people who had unneeded items had a few options for disposing of them. They could hold a garage sale, which involved organizing and sorting items, sitting around all day, and hoping that someone who needed the items happened by. Another option was to place a newspaper ad, which involved paying money with no guarantee of a sale, and hoping that a local buyer who needed the item happened to read the tiny ad in the back of the paper. Other options included hanging fliers, going to a pawnshop, or donating the items to charity.

Prior to the advent of eBay and Craigslist, the odds of finding a buyer who needed and wanted an item you had to sell were low. Finding the person who was willing to pay the most for that item was even more difficult. Countless valuable antiques, comic books, baseball cards, and other collectibles, along with needed items such as baby strollers, sporting goods, and children's clothes, have been sold for pennies on the dollar simply because there was no good way to find buyers.

Craigslist, eBay, and other online marketplaces have changed all of this. For a fee, sellers can put an item on eBay, allowing bidders around the world to face off against each other to get the item. A rare item, such as an old comic book that might have fetched little at a garage sale, might spark a bidding war among collectors who could raise the price to hundreds or thousands of dollars by the time the auction closes. Arguably, such a sale might benefit sellers more than buyers, but many collectors would rather spend their weekends doing something other than traveling from one garage sale or flea market to another.

For more mundane items, such as clothes that children have outgrown; strollers, cribs, and other baby gear; sporting goods; bicycles; and furniture, Craigslist offers sellers a means of reaching a large number of buyers who can automatically monitor the site for needed items. The online marketplace brings together sellers (such parents of older children) and buyers (such as new parents) in a manner that is convenient for both parties. Sellers do not have to waste time or money on advertising or holding a garage sale, and buyers do not have to waste time reading the newspaper hoping to find what they are looking for.

In economic terms, online marketplaces reduce transaction costs. When you purchase an item, you are paying not just for the item, but the costs to get that item to you. It might cost a farmer very little to grow a tomato. If you visited the farm and asked to buy a tomato, the farmer might be able to sell you a tomato for much less than it would cost in the supermarket and still make a nice profit. When you buy that tomato at a supermarket, however, there are a number of costs that result in you paying much more than you would pay the farmer. The tomato has to be transported to the store; the store must pay rent, electrical bills, and employee wages; the store advertises tomatoes in its weekly newspaper ad; and even the process of planning where to buy the tomatoes to sell in the store involves time and effort.

Online marketplaces have few transaction costs to the buyer or seller. There are minimal costs associated with electricity and Internet access, which buyer and seller usually maintain for other purposes anyway. There are costs associated with mailing (gas and postage) or going to pick up an item (gas). While Craigslist is usually free, eBay charges fees based on listing an item, selling an item, and transferring money through its payment service. Online transactions, however, are quick for both the buyer and seller. For high-volume sellers, an eBay store is more efficient, because there is no need to maintain a "brick and mortar" store, fewer (or no) employees are needed, and shoplifting is not a concern. When transaction costs are reduced, buyers and sellers benefit because profits can be higher even though buyers pay less.

What happens, however, when transaction costs are also reduced for illegitimate transactions, such as those involving stolen or counterfeit merchandise? Arguably, reduced transaction costs for such transactions would make them more commonplace. While legislation has been directed at preventing fake medications, perfumes, clothing, CDs, DVDs, etc., from being sold online, the issue of addressing the sale of stolen goods is more complex. In recent years, some members of Congress have introduced "e-fencing" (stealing stolen merchandise is known as "fencing") laws, which through a variety of legal mechanisms are intended to limit online transactions in such a way as to make the sale of stolen goods more difficult. Online retailers have pressured Congress to pass legislation in response to the problem of "organized retail crime," in which groups systematically steal high-value merchandise, sometimes returning it for store credit, and then sell the merchandise or store credits.

Not surprisingly, online marketplaces such as eBay and Craigslist have fought restrictions on e-fencing. Online marketplaces do not dispute that some percentage of merchandise sold through auctions or classified ads is stolen. That said, they do not think the answer to this problem is placing limits on all sellers of merchandise. The proposed e-fencing laws would require sites such as eBay and Craigslist to investigate sellers and remove listings at the request of a retailer who believes that the seller is offering stolen merchandise. The editorial board of the Newark *Star-Ledger* criticized such legislation: "The auction sites would have to snoop on sellers to sniff out transactions that might involve stolen goods whenever a retailer asked, even if the retailer merely suspected something about an offer was dicey because of a low price. This would be an impossible burden."[2]

In addition to putting unnecessary burdens on the operators of auction sites, critics say, restrictions would also burden the vast majority of sellers who are honest people and simply want to turn unneeded items into cash. Steve DelBianco, the director of the trade group NetChoice that represents online marketplaces such as eBay, told a congressional committee that many honest people do not maintain documents that prove their ownership of personal items, so requiring documentation in order to sell items online is simply unfair. Criticizing three proposed laws, he said:

> All three of these bills would give retailers unique new power to force an online marketplace to interrogate their own customers about how they obtained the item they are listing for sale. This has the effect of presuming that their customers and sellers are selling stolen items unless they can prove their ownership. How could a seller prove ownership of something they have received as a gift, in a trade for cash or something for which they have lost the receipts a long time ago? The vast majority of online sellers are honest people trying to find the highest bidder for something they have and don't need or something they have acquired legally at a discounted price.
>
> Honest citizens are understandably going to resent having to provide receipts and personal information to prove that they are not involved in organized criminal activity.[3]

While these laws might help reduce the flow of stolen goods on the Internet, they will also raise the operating costs of auction and classified sites. Ultimately, critics say, the increased costs will come out of consumers' wallets. On its blog, the trade group NetChoice declared:

Organized Retail Crime Act of 2008, H.R. 6941, 110th Congress, 2nd Session.

The following is an excerpt from one of several bills whose sponsors proposed to limit the sale of goods on online marketplaces such as eBay. Retailers say these measures are needed to protect their property rights, while online marketplaces say they are an attempt to stifle competition:

It is unlawful for an operator of an online marketplace to fail to—

(1) expeditiously investigate when credible evidence of sales of goods or services acquired through organized retail crime on its online marketplace comes to its attention, and remove from the online marketplace or disable access to material from the online marketplace of sellers offering goods or services when the result of the investigation provides knowledge or a reasonable cause to know that the goods or services were acquired through organized retail crime, and maintain a record of all investigations for a minimum of three years;

(2) require the seller of property whose merchandise packaging identifies the property as being available from a particular or exclusive retail source, to post such identifying information conspicuously on the Internet site where other information about the property is posted; and

(3) in the case of each high volume seller—

(A) maintain the following information for three years—

(i) the name, telephone number, e-mail address, legitimate physical address, any user identification, and company name of the high-volume seller; and

(ii) all transactions conducted by each high-volume seller on the online marketplace for the most recent three-year period; and

(B) require any high-volume seller to—

(i) conspicuously post its name, telephone number, and legitimate address on the Internet site where other information about the property being sold by the high-volume seller is posted; or

(ii) provide, upon request of any business that has a reasonable suspicion that goods or services at the site were acquired through organized retail crime, its name, telephone number, and legitimate physical address.

Unfortunately, the people that these bills would hit the hardest are not the criminals; they are the American consumers who have come to rely on Internet-based small businesses to find good products at great prices, which in this difficult economy, is needed now more than ever.[4]

eBay and other auction sites allow small businesses to prosper.

While eBay, Amazon.com, and several online marketplaces have become large, successful companies, they are also the public face of thousands of small businesses. In addition to sellers of collectibles such as Troy Thoreson, online marketplaces also serve as the home of small businesses that seek bargains on unused merchandise and then sell them online for bargain prices.

Most of these discount sellers are legitimate businesses. They obtain merchandise cheaply, such as when a store goes out of business or when a manufacturer discontinues a product or simply has too much of it in stock. Others might purchase soon-to-expire pharmaceutical products such as over-the-counter medications, vitamins, and diabetic testing strips. Admittedly, not all sellers are honest, and some stolen merchandise is also sold at prices much lower than those offered in stores or at "traditional" online retailers such as Target or Walgreens. Online marketplaces, however, prohibit such activities and suspend sellers' privileges for selling stolen merchandise.

In fact, Target, Walgreens, Home Depot, and other major retailers have been key supporters of "e-fencing" bills, both in Congress and in state legislatures. One of the key complaints about the proposed legislation is that it would help these large retailers drive their smaller, online-only competitors out of business. It should be noted that these retailers also operate their own Web sites, which are in direct competition with eBay, Amazon.com, and other auction and classified sites.

NetChoice's DelBianco criticized a proposed law that would enable retailers to demand that online marketplaces turn over information about sellers or block sales of suspected stolen merchandise. He said the proposal would be

> handing competing retailers a blunt instrument to harass online marketplaces they compete with. A stereo retailer, for instance, could tell Amazon or eBay, "Those speakers are listed so cheap that I just KNOW they are stolen." Never mind that big-box retailers fill our weekend newspapers with ads offering deep discounts to draw shoppers into their stores, too.[5]

DelBianco warned members of Congress that e-fencing laws that enabled retailers to demand investigations of sellers

eBay Policies Regarding Stolen Property

eBay strictly forbids the sale of stolen property, which violates state, federal and international law. eBay strongly supports law enforcement efforts to recover stolen property that is listed on its Web site, and urges the prosecution of those responsible for knowingly attempting to sell such items on eBay.

eBay forbids its members from listing goods that have altered or removed serial numbers, as the possession and sale of such items is prohibited in a majority of states in the U.S.

Violations of this policy may result in a range of actions, including:

- Listing cancellation
- Limits on account privileges
- Account suspension
- Forfeit of eBay fees on cancelled listings
- Loss of PowerSeller status

Source: http://pages.ebay.com/help/policies/stolen.html.

or removal of listings would lead to abuse. He was especially concerned about a proposed law that would allow retailers to demand action by online marketplaces any time within a year of a theft reported to police, without any additional involvement by law enforcement. Such a situation would allow traditional retailers to harass their online competitors, he argued:

> Think for a moment about a small retail store manager who is trying to maintain margins in a declining economy . . . if a batch of items are stolen from his store and he later sees the same items, similar items, online, he is going to pull the trigger . . . [and] force the online marketplace to interrogate its seller. And the retailer has no cost, he has no downside at all, and he can actually reuse the same investigation notice over and over again for every listing he sees on the Internet.[6]

Owners of merchandise, not online marketplaces, are responsible for preventing theft.

Essentially, retailers would like Congress to transfer the cost of preventing merchandise theft from themselves to online retailers because they see retail crime as a crime of opportunity: It is easy to sell stolen merchandise online, and it is also easy to sell credit-card-like store credits that can be gotten by "returning" shoplifted items. Retailers therefore argue that sites such as eBay and Craigslist are creating a reason for people to shoplift and thus must bear the costs of preventing such theft.

Critics of e-fencing laws, however, ridicule the notion that the ease of selling merchandise on Craigslist, eBay, and other online marketplaces encourages crime. The *Star-Ledger*'s editorial board suggested, "The idea that online auctions are insidiously turning masses of law-abiding citizens into crooks is about as valid as the belief that getting the car washed creates harmonic vibrations in the atmosphere that produce rain."[7] In reality, online marketplaces are only one avenue for fencing

In testimony given before the House Subcommittee on Crime on June 14, 2001, eBay vice president and deputy general counsel Robert Chesnut (*right*) claimed that "the Internet provides law enforcement and private businesses so many opportunities to fight crime with creative solutions, many of which could exist only because of the Internet."

stolen goods. Robert Chesnut, a security executive with eBay, reminded a congressional committee that the committee's own research had identified a wide array of marketplaces for stolen goods, including "small shops (including beauty shops, gas stations, music stores, bars and gyms), flea markets, pawnshops, local fences, truck stops, newspaper ads, overseas buyers, and yes, the Internet through all types of web sites and chat forums."[8]

At another hearing, DelBianco argued that retailers were trying to make online marketplaces responsible for preventing retail theft, when in fact retailers are in a much better position to prevent the theft that is taking place in their stores. He noted that the representative of a grocery chain had testified "our associates are there to sell groceries, not to be police officers," and the same witness and another retailer's representative had "stressed the importance of limiting and deterring theft 'in the first place.' "[9] DelBianco felt that the retailers were trying to escape responsibility: "The first place that theft occurs is in their own stores. . . . Rather than shifting blame and burdens to online marketplaces, retailers should improve their employee screening, inventory control measures, and store security systems."[10]

In his testimony, DelBianco also noted that the retailers' own employees were responsible for much of the theft, and that to hold a third party such as eBay or Craigslist responsible was misguided:

> The National Retail Federation's own commissioned surveys, conducted annually by the University of Florida, consistently show that two-thirds of retailer inventory losses are directly attributable to internal causes, including theft by their own employees and suppliers. Year after year, about half of all retail inventory losses are the result of employee theft. To put this in a national context, the retailers' own study concluded that "there is no other form of larceny that annually costs American citizens more money than employee theft."
>
> These are the retailers' own employees, people who are hired, managed, and paid by the retailers. With that kind of direct control, retailers are in the position to stop employee theft where it starts.[11]

Laws singling out online marketplaces are unnecessary.

Inherent in the argument that retailers, rather than online retailers, should be responsible for preventing retail theft is the recognition that stealing merchandise and selling it online are already illegal activities. E-fencing laws, however, put administrative burdens on online marketplaces that other marketplaces do not face.

Unlike the thief selling stolen car stereos in a back alley, selling merchandise in an online marketplace leaves the electronic equivalent of a "paper trail." When a complaint is filed with police, detectives can access information from online marketplaces that can help to solve the crime. For example, police in Fort Lauderdale, Florida, were able to retrieve items stolen from the International Swimming Hall of Fame after the items were listed for sale on eBay. A janitor temporarily working at the hall of fame allegedly stole some valuable historical items, including Olympic memorabilia that once belonged to Johnny Weissmuller and Buster Crabbe, famous U.S. swimmers who both went on to play Tarzan in movies. The janitor then tried to sell Olympic medals and other items on eBay. A collector, curious as to why the hall of fame would part with such an important part of swimming history, sent an inquiry to the hall's staff. The Fort Lauderdale Police Department then set up a "sting" operation to purchase memorabilia from the janitor, allowing them to arrest him and recover many of the stolen items.

In arguing against e-fencing laws, eBay's management has pointed out the many ways that the company has tried to prevent the sale of stolen merchandise. The eBay site touts some of the company's initiatives, including training more than 20,000 law enforcement officers nationwide on how to prevent, detect, and punish sales of stolen merchandise. Additionally, the company maintains a database of items that are sold by high-volume "drop-off" stores—stores at which merchandise can be dropped off for sale on eBay—and law enforcement agencies can monitor this database to seek out stolen items. In all, the company has 1,000 employees devoted to keeping eBay free of illegal activity.

Summary

Nobody is quite sure how much stolen merchandise is sold on online marketplaces such as eBay and Craigslist, but most "e-commerce" supporters say that it is a miniscule percentage. The retail industry, however, says that those sales are a direct attack on their bottom line and therefore have pushed a number of e-fencing laws that would make it more difficult for thieves to sell their wares online. Such laws have met with great resistance because they increase the cost of doing business online and unfairly single out just one of the many avenues through which stolen goods are disposed. The low cost and convenience of online marketplaces benefit buyers and sellers, and supporters of e-commerce argue that restrictions would ultimately hurt small businesses and consumers. They argue that existing laws are sufficient for prosecuting theft and that retailers, not online marketplaces, bear the responsibility for preventing retail theft.

Laws Are Needed to Curb Sales of Stolen Merchandise Online

Bruce and Laura Wasz owned several pawnshops in the Chicago area. Traditionally, pawnshops—legal businesses to which people can bring jewelry, stereos, sporting goods, bicycles, musical instruments, and other valuable items and receive cash in return—have been a popular outlet for thieves. States, however, have developed increasingly strict laws to prevent this type of activity. For the Waszes, the Internet presented a new opportunity to make money without facing harsh restrictions. In fact, it was such a great opportunity that they were no longer willing to wait for thieves to come to them.

The Waszes, mother and son, were convicted of selling more than $1 million worth of tools, appliances, and hardware stolen from home improvement centers. They made arrangements with a group of thieves who had specialized in stealing merchandise from stores such as Home Depot. The thieves had been returning the stolen items for cash or store credit, but store policies were making it more difficult to do this. Therefore, the ring of thieves arranged with the Waszes to sell the stolen merchandise on eBay, using their pawnshops as a front. By specializing in specific merchandise, such as tankless water heaters and sump pumps, the Waszes were able to build favorable reputations with buyers of these items. To the naïve purchaser, the Waszes seemed to offer great deals and good service.

A sump pump manufacturer, however, was not quite as impressed with the Waszes as their eBay customers were. In fact, the manufacturer was quite suspicious as to how the Waszes could be selling brand-new merchandise at prices lower than what the manufacturer charged retailers. This type of "undercutting" hurts not only the retailers whose merchandise is stolen, but also the manufacturer. When a product is sold inexpensively on the Internet, legitimate retailers are pressured to lower their prices, and the manufacturer is in turn pressured to lower the wholesale prices it charges to retailers.

By the time the Federal Bureau of Investigation (FBI) was able to stop the scheme, however, the Waszes and their co-conspirators had stolen a considerable amount of merchandise. In addition to hitting Chicago-area home improvement warehouses, the thieves traveled to Colorado, Maryland, Michigan, Minnesota, Missouri, New Jersey, Ohio, Tennessee, Virginia, and Wisconsin to steal merchandise specified by the Waszes. By that point, unsuspecting people throughout the country had bought stolen merchandise from what they thought was a legitimate merchant.

Many major retailers support laws that would make it more difficult for a scheme such as this to succeed. Retailers such as Home Depot, Target, and Walgreens, however, are not the only ones that support e-fencing legislation. Rare-book collectors have spoken out in favor of the laws, not wanting to see precious books sold by thieves, or even worse, cut up to be sold as color prints on eBay. Musicians who have had their favorite instruments stolen want to be able to prevent thieves from unloading them on Craigslist. Of course, many law enforcement officials support e-fencing laws because many honest people end up receiving stolen goods.

Online marketplaces make it too profitable to fence stolen merchandise.

A major problem with online marketplaces such as eBay and Craigslist, retailers say, is that they present too much temptation to people such as the Waszes. Although they were selling products for a fraction of the retail cost, the Waszes were still taking advantage of eBay's auction process, which pits buyer against buyer and drives up the price. They were also expanding their pool of customers across the country. As Brad Brekke, a loss prevention official with Target, testified before Congress: "Fencing stolen goods used to be a local face-to-face process in which buyers and sellers were limited and operations were only marginally profitable."[1] An article in the *Washington Post* noted that while shoplifters typically get about 10 cents on the dollar for stolen merchandise, a shoplifting ring that turned to selling on eBay was netting 76 cents on the dollar before being busted by authorities.[2]

Why is such a criminal operation so profitable? The Internet presents an affordable way to reach millions of potential buyers. Just as the low cost of doing business on the Internet benefits both legitimate sellers and their customers, it has also become a boon to sellers of stolen merchandise. The low prices are irresistible to buyers, even those who should realize that the prices are too low to be legitimate. Joseph LaRocca of the National Retail Federation, which represents traditional retailers, told Congress that the lure of making quick money is an inducement to break the law:

> The Internet seems to be contributing to the creation of a brand new type of retail thief—people who have never stolen before, but are lured in by the convenience

and anonymity of the Internet. . . . In videotaped admissions of people who have stolen from retail stores and resold the product on e-Bay, for example, thieves often tell the same disturbing story: they begin legitimately selling product on e-Bay and then become "hooked" by its addictive qualities, the anonymity it provides, and the ease with which they gain exposure to millions of customers. When they run out of "legitimate merchandise," they begin to steal intermittently, many times for the first time in their life, so they can continue selling online. The thefts then begin to spiral out of control and, before they know it, they quit their jobs, are recruiting accomplices (some are even hiring "boosters"), and are crossing state lines to steal—all so they can support and perpetuate their online selling habit. At least one major retailer has reported that 80 percent of thieves interviewed in their e-Bay theft cases admit that selling stolen property on e-Bay is their sole source of income. In fact, many of the e-Bay sellers have used those proceeds to obtain mortgages, new cars, and even boats.[3]

The ease and anonymity of selling online makes it almost impossible to prevent stolen goods from making it to market.

An interesting aspect of the Wasz case discussed at the beginning of this chapter is that the thieves turned to the Waszes to help them sell merchandise on eBay after retailers began to crack down on their previous scheme, which was to steal merchandise and return it for cash. Perhaps fearing detection, the thieves worked with the Waszes, who were able to quickly and anonymously make the merchandise available. Rather than selling the merchandise in their stores, the Waszes turned to eBay, using a number of aliases to sell the stolen merchandise. Among the aliases the Waszes used were "amolaur," "beewasz," "goldrush," "gooddeal1010," and "sellya1."

The ability to set up such aliases and therefore remain unknown to retailers and law enforcement officials has been most irksome to supporters of e-fencing legislation. U.S. Representative Bobby Scott of Virginia lamented:

> Traditionally, thieves who dispose of stolen goods locally through flea markets, pawnshops, swap meets or shady storefront operations where State and local police can investigate and make arrests, as the thieves have to physically stand behind the stolen goods. But without having to identify themselves or their contact information to consumers or others who seek information about them, OTRs that operate online evade

E-Fencing Enforcement Act of 2008, H.R. 6713

Critics say that it is too easy to get away with selling stolen property on eBay. Bills such as the E-Fencing Enforcement Act of 2008 would give more power to victims of theft to prevent their property from being sold online. The following is an excerpt from the proposed bill:

(a) Duty To Provide Information—It shall be the duty of each online marketplace provider to disclose contact information for any high volume seller to any inquirer with standing under this section to seek that information.

(b) Duty To Retain Information About High Volume Sellers—It shall be the duty of each online marketplace provider to retain contact information for three years after receipt of that information from high volume seller.

(c) Take-Down Requirement—Upon the request of a recipient of contact information under this section, it shall be the duty of the provider to determine, based on information reasonably available to it or that could be obtained by the provider without undue expense, whether the goods or items were lawfully acquired. If the provider determines that there is good reason to believe the goods or items were unlawfully acquired, it shall be the duty of the provider to preclude access by the high volume seller to the online marketplace with respect to those goods or items.

identification much easier than traditional thieves, and they put themselves beyond the reach of local law enforcement.[4]

Scott was speaking in support of legislation that would require online marketplaces such as eBay to reveal the actual name, physical address, phone number, and e-mail address of any seller with more than $12,000 in annual sales, rather than allowing them to hide behind aliases such as "amolaur."

While eBay has cooperated with law enforcement agencies, its approach has generally been to intervene only after police get involved. Retailers say this approach is ineffective, because the volume of goods stolen from retailers would make it impossible to prosecute every case. In fact, Target's Brad Brekke noted that the retailing giant apprehends about 75,000 thieves per year, while the entire caseload of federal prosecutors is only about 60,000 cases. Brekke argued that eBay and other sites need to do more to stop stolen goods from getting to market:

> We need Internet auction sites to make simple changes that deter the sale of stolen property. The simple step of requiring high volume Internet sellers to identify themselves and add a unique product identifier, such as serial numbers to their listings, would permit identification and tracing of stolen property. It would also effectively constrain the sale of stolen property without additional law enforcement involvement.[5]

Brekke noted that similar measures are proven deterrents: "In fact, every vehicle listed for sale on eBay motors is now accompanied by a VIN number. This has virtually eliminated the sale of stolen vehicles on eBay," he said.[6]

A loss-prevention official with Walgreens, the national pharmacy chain, emphasized the importance of enacting laws that would help to prevent e-fencing rather than simply prosecuting it after the fact. He testified:

In Texas, Walgreens and other retailers collaborated with law enforcement on a case that involved a fence who was buying $50,000 to $100,000 worth of stolen baby formula, diabetic test strips and other over-the-counter medications every single day. The stolen product was being stored in a mini warehouse with no temperature controls in an area where temperatures routinely exceed 100 degrees during the summer months. The merchandise was being sold back to unsuspecting retailers and fenced over the Internet. This type of activity puts the public's health and safety at risk as merchandise like baby formula and OTC medications can easily degrade.[7]

The market for merchandise and gift cards has fueled organized retail crime.

In general, buying merchandise on eBay, Craigslist, and other online marketplaces is considered socially acceptable. Many people who would never consider purchasing an iPod in a back alley, at a barbershop, or from someone selling them out of a car trunk might consider buying an iPod at below retail cost on eBay. Supporters of e-fencing legislation say that the inclusion of stolen merchandise in a generally legitimate marketplace has the effect of increasing demand.

As consumers grow accustomed to getting bargains on eBay, Craigslist, and other sites, demand for bargains increases. In difficult economic times, consumers demand bargains on items such as the latest video game players, designer handbags, GPS systems, and MP3 players. The National Retail Federation's LaRocca told Reuters news service, "The demand for product at a reduced price is significantly up. Consumers are looking at alternative resources to find products. Unfortunately, consumers and the economy are fueling a drive for this illegal or anonymous commerce that is taking place across the country."[8]

In effect, supporters of e-fencing legislation say, eBay and other online marketplaces actually fuel crime. In rejecting the

Waszes' appeal of their prison sentences, the court noted the pawnbrokers' role in giving their co-defendants motivation to commit more thefts:

> Vis-à-vis their thieving co-defendants, the Waszes provided an outlet for the stolen merchandise that the thieves sorely needed. Due to changes in the merchandise return policies of their retailer victims, the thieving co-defendants were finding it increasingly difficult to steal goods and then return the items to the stores for cash refunds. As the owners of pawnshops, the Waszes had a ready-made cover for the handling of stolen merchandise. By agreeing to buy the stolen merchandise from the thieves and sell it on eBay, the Waszes enabled their co-defendants to circumvent the problem of store returns, supplied them with a guaranteed income on their thefts, and in these ways enabled their co-defendants to continue stealing and to do so on a relatively large-scale basis.[9]

Neither the private sector nor local law enforcement has stemmed the problems.

In objecting to e-fencing legislation, eBay has launched a legislative and public relations campaign touting its cooperation with law enforcement. Retailers suffering losses of stolen merchandise, however, believe that eBay's efforts at self-policing are inadequate. On eBay, sellers offer merchandise that a reasonable person should know to be stolen—many sellers such as the Waszes offer large quantities of merchandise at prices below the wholesale prices charged by manufacturers. However, eBay does not make these assumptions about its sellers. Nor does the company respond to requests made by retailers directly to eBay. Instead, eBay acts when contacted by law enforcement officials. In addition to making it difficult to prevent stolen goods from being sold, critics say, the requirement that law enforcement officials initiate requests relies on overburdened police forces to investigate shoplifting, which is often a low-priority crime.

One of the reasons that retailers have supported federal e-fencing legislation is that selling merchandise over the Internet is not a local problem but a national one. For example, the Waszes sold merchandise stolen in a number of other states, but law enforcement agencies from those states would have had difficulty investigating and prosecuting the Waszes in their home state of Illinois. As Jack Trlica, the editor of *Loss Prevention* magazine, observed, "Although state and local law enforcement track, apprehend, and prosecute these crimes when they uncover them, they are often unable to pursue these criminals thoroughly, if at all, because jurisdictional limitations prevent it . . . and criminals know it."[10]

State laws typically consider theft of merchandise of less than a certain dollar value to be a misdemeanor (a less serious

eBay's Instructions for Reporting Stolen Property

As of press time, eBay has a policy of not responding directly to reports of stolen items submitted by the general public. Instead, a police report must be filed, and law enforcement officials must contact eBay:

Theft of Property: If members see an item on eBay that they believe is stolen, the best course is to contact law enforcement immediately. Under eBay's privacy rules, eBay's attorneys will provide important records about pending and past listings with an official request from law enforcement officials. eBay will ask that members inform the police officer handling the case that eBay will be pleased to cooperate in the investigation, and ask the officer to contact eBay using eBay's law enforcement-specific webform. The officer should include all relevant information, including the case number and any item numbers or User IDs.

Source: http://pages.ebay.com/help/policies/stolen.html.

crime not carrying a long prison sentence), and therefore some criminals plan their crimes so that they stay under that dollar amount. As Trlica explains, the ability to manipulate these laws makes prosecuting organized retail crime (ORC) rings much more difficult:

> Ultimately, the Internet is a boundary-less marketplace that affords criminals access to an endless supply of unwitting buyers. State laws were not designed to combat this. Criminals have thrived because of this patchwork of state laws and will only be deterred if Congress passes a federal ORC statute with teeth.[11]

Summary

Sites such as eBay and Craigslist have many benefits, linking buyers and sellers of used items, and also enabling legitimate businesses to sell items at lower costs. These same low costs, however, make online marketplaces attractive to thieves, who can make a much larger profit disposing of stolen merchandise online than they can by selling it on the street. So great are the profits that some sellers are turning to theft rings, specifying the merchandise they want to sell. As more merchandise becomes available at bargain prices, consumers will begin to expect such bargains online, and the growth of the black market will further fuel theft.

The Benefits of Online Pharmacies Far Outweigh the Risks

Recent court rulings have required that women 17 and older have access without a prescription to the "morning-after pill," or "Plan B," a form of birth control pill that can be taken after unprotected sex to prevent a pregnancy. Before the rulings, the morning-after pill had required a doctor's prescription. Many women, however, had difficulties obtaining prescriptions. For some, access was made difficult by a physician's moral objections to the pill, which many doctors believe aborts an embryo shortly after an egg and sperm are united. For example, a 50-year-old woman had unprotected sex for the first time in more than 20 years and called her gynecologist to ask for a prescription for the morning-after pill; the gynecologist told her that she did not write prescriptions for the morning-after pill. For others, access was difficult because of the timing of the incident. A college-bound young woman unwisely had unprotected sex and was not sure where to turn because she had just moved to a new town and did not have a health care provider. Another woman had unprotected sex over the weekend, after her doctor's office had closed, and was concerned about waiting until Monday to be seen by a doctor. Sometimes personal reasons made seeking a prescription for Plan B uncomfortable. For example, an Illinois nurse who had a working relationship with local physicians did not want to have to tell one of them that she had had unprotected sex.

For each of these women, the solution was the Internet. They used a site that has been featured in publications such as *Cosmopolitan, Glamour,* the *Wall Street Journal, Maxim,* and *Salon.* The site allows women to pay a $25 fee and receive an online consultation with a licensed physician, who then faxes or calls a prescription in to the pharmacy of the woman's choice. The confidential procedure can be much more comfortable for women already under stress and possibly embarrassed, and it is available when doctors' offices are closed. In the words of one reviewer, some women "feel much more comfortable talking [about having had unprotected sex] to Dr. Internet than to Dr. Disapproval."[1]

Online medical consultations have many benefits to consumers.

In the United States, all medications must be approved by a federal agency called the Food and Drug Administration (FDA). The FDA decides whether to approve a medication based on scientific testing, typically conducted by a drug's manufacturer, with the assistance of universities and hospitals. Generally, a drug's manufacturer must show that the drug is safe and effective at treating a particular disease or condition.

Drugs are generally divided into two categories: prescription and nonprescription medications. To obtain a prescription medication legally, you must have a written, oral, or electronic order from a medical professional (usually a physician or a nurse practitioner), and the medication must be dispensed by a licensed pharmacist, who receives extensive training in medications and must be able to answer any questions that you might have about the medication. Most drugs used to treat serious medical conditions or infections are available only by prescription. For example, a person would need a prescription for medications used to treat high blood pressure, diabetes, or mental illness. In the United States, a prescription is also required for antibiotics to treat bacterial infections, for drugs used to treat erectile dysfunction, and birth control pills. Within the class of prescription drugs are certain "controlled substances," such as the pain medication OxyContin. The federal government further limits who can write prescriptions for the medications and how they are dispensed by pharmacies. The additional controls are necessary because the drugs have the potential to be abused by patients or sold as "street drugs."

Federal Investigative Report Identifies Three Types of Online Pharmacies

Three general types of Internet pharmacies sell prescription drugs directly to consumers:

First, some Internet pharmacies operate much like traditional drugstores, selling a wide range of prescription drugs and requiring consumers to submit a prescription from their physicians before their orders are filled. In some instances, these Internet pharmacies are affiliated with traditional chain stores.

Second, other Internet pharmacies may sell a more limited range of drugs, often specializing in certain lifestyle medications, such as those that treat sexual dysfunction or assist in weight control. These Internet pharmacies typically require consumers to fill out an online medical history questionnaire in place of a traditional examination by a physician, and issue a prescription after a physician affiliated with the pharmacy reviews the questionnaire.

Still other Internet pharmacies dispense drugs without a prescription.

Source: U.S. General Accounting Office, "Internet Pharmacies: Some Pose Safety Risks to Consumers," GAO-04-820 (June 2004), p. 8.

Nonprescription drugs, by contrast, can be purchased easily at drugstores, supermarkets, convenience stores, and even in vending machines. Some medications once available by prescription only are now available "over the counter," that is, without a prescription. Two common examples are the pain reliever ibuprofen, sometimes sold under the Advil name brand, and the allergy medication loratadine, sold as Claritin. Some medications that require a prescription in the United States do not require a prescription in other countries. Additionally, the morning-after pills discussed in the introduction to the chapter are now available without a prescription, enabling women to access emergency contraception without the cost, inconvenience, and delay of a doctors' visit.

Many relatively safe medications for easily diagnosed conditions continue to require a prescription. Examples include erectile dysfunction drugs such as Cialis, Levitra, and Viagra, male baldness remedies such as Propecia, and smoking-cessation aids such as Chantix. Many people want to use the Internet as a convenient, anonymous way to obtain these drugs without visiting a doctor's office, and a number of Web sites make these medications readily available. The legality of such Web sites, however is questionable because of a patchwork of state and federal laws.

Proponents of legalizing online prescribing based on the results of a questionnaire say that the practice is safe and has many benefits for consumers. As discussed in the introduction, some people feel uncomfortable talking about certain issues with their personal physicians; they might need medications at a time when a physician visit is inconvenient or impossible; or they might not currently have a health care provider. One operator of an online pharmacy told *Fortune* magazine that while physical examinations by doctors are essential to preserving health, his belief is that "20% to 50% of all physician visits are unnecessary."[2]

In testimony to Congress, Philadelphia lawyer Patrick Egan, who specializes in health and criminal defense law, discussed some of the additional benefits of online prescribing. Criticizing a law restricting online distribution of prescription medications without a prior prescription, Egan said that online prescribing was an innovation that could reduce the cost of health care for millions of Americans, such as people living in rural and frontier areas:

> Americans [who] live in nonmetropolitan areas have substandard access to physicians and have no other alternative than to forgo medical care and prescription drug use or make costly trips to doctors in other counties. . . . "Online pharmacies" that do not need "valid prescriptions" enable these individuals to receive prescription medicine at a reasonable cost. The "online

The Marketing of Prescription Drugs Through Online Prescribing

Many Web sites offer prescription drugs for sale to people who do not already have a prescription for the drug. These sites typically ask the user to submit medical information, which is then reviewed by a physician who issues a prescription. The following language appears on hundreds of Web sites:

> If you have had a physical exam recently and consider yourself healthy, you do not necessarily require another physical exam in order for you to obtain the medications we offer. Thousands of psychiatrists and general practitioners throughout the US are prescribing certain medications after only reviewing the patient's medical history, without a physical exam. The medical factors that would prohibit a physician from prescribing these medications are discoverable through a review of the patient's medical history. There is no reason to suggest that an in-person review of this history is any more relevant than an online consultation.

Sources: http://www.pharmacydrugs.natureflower.com/; http://www.viagragroup.com/faq. htm; http://www.no-prescription-pharmacy.com/about.htm; and 499 other Web sites.

pharmacy" is a new innovation that would avail individuals in nonmetropolitan areas access to healthcare and reduce the deterrent effect to seeking healthcare.[3]

Egan also noted that online pharmacies might be the only reasonable alternative for millions of Americans without health insurance:

> Uninsured Americans are more likely to forgo the use of medical care and prescription drugs. These individuals are three times as likely not to have had a doctor's visit in the last three years. The Proposed Bill would foreclose any chance for the uninsured population to receive medical care and prescription medicines. The ability for the uninsured to purchase cheaper medications from U.S. "online pharamacies" without a "valid prescription" is a valid option for the uninsured to obtain prescription medicine. If the uninsured were forced to go to doctors [in person] to get a "valid prescription," the uninsured would not go at all because these individuals can clearly not afford medical care.[4]

The Ryan Haight Act of 2008 went too far in restricting sales of controlled substances.

The bill that Egan was criticizing eventually became a federal law, the Ryan Haight Act, in 2008. While issuing any prescription on the basis of an online consultation has been controversial, the congressional debates focused on the online prescribing of certain types of drugs that had high potential for abuse: drugs such as the painkillers OxyContin and Vicodin, barbiturates such as Valium and Xanax, and stimulants such as Ritalin. These drugs are often used as street drugs to get "high" and have a strong potential for addiction.

Earlier versions of the law were much stricter than the law that ultimately passed. In 2005, two senators, Norm Coleman and Dianne Feinstein, introduced a bill that stated that, in general, "a person may not dispense a prescription drug . . . [if] the purchaser communicated with the person through the Internet . . . [and] the patient for whom the drug was dispensed or purchased did not, when such communications began, have a prescription for the drug that is valid in the United States" unless the person subsequently obtained a prescription from a medical professional who (or whose partner) had conducted "at least one in-person medical evaluation of the patient."[5]

Although the final law prohibited online prescribing of controlled substances only, some critics, such as Egan, suggest that even these restrictions go too far. Noting that painkillers and diet pills are vitally important to many people who might be unable to visit a doctor for financial or other reasons, Egan testified to Congress:

> The Proposed Bill directly impacts the ability of Americans to treat chronic pain, which affects up to 85 percent of adults at some point in their lives, and obesity, which affects 66 percent of the population. An estimated 300,000 premature deaths are caused by obesity each year, while an estimated 146,377 deaths from the period 1979–1998 [were] caused by arthritis. We do not seek to marginalize the 26,000 citizens who die from the total effects of all drugs each year (nonmedical use of prescription medicine included); however, for the greater public good, the ability to purchase prescription medication from "online pharmacies" without the need to visit a doctor far outweighs the cost to society.[6]

Extending regulations beyond controlled substances is unnecessary.

While Congress backed down from banning online prescriptions for the vast majority of drugs that are not considered controlled substances, the legality of the practice remains murky. In each

THE LETTER OF THE LAW

Ryan Haight Online Pharmacy Consumer Protection Act of 2008

Public Law No. 110-425, 110th Congress, 2nd session (October 15, 2008)

In 2008, President George W. Bush signed a law prohibiting the prescribing of controlled substances based on an Internet consultation by a doctor who had not seen the patient in person. An exception was made for doctors who practice as a group, so that if one doctor was on vacation, for example, another doctor in his or her medical practice could prescribe a controlled substance to the patient. The following is an excerpt from the bill:

(1) No controlled substance that is a prescription drug as determined under the Federal Food, Drug, and Cosmetic Act may be delivered, distributed, or dispensed by means of the Internet without a valid prescription.

   (2) As used in this subsection:

      (A) The term "valid prescription" means a prescription that is issued for a legitimate medical purpose in the usual course of professional practice by—

         (i) a practitioner who has conducted at least 1 in-person medical evaluation of the patient; or

         (ii) a covering practitioner.

      (B) (i) The term "in-person medical evaluation" means a medical evaluation that is conducted with the patient in the physical presence of the practitioner....

      (C) The term "covering practitioner" means, with respect to a patient, a practitioner who conducts a medical evaluation (other than an in-person medical evaluation) at the request of a practitioner who—

         (i) has conducted at least 1 in-person medical evaluation of the patient or an evaluation of the patient through the practice of telemedicine, within the previous 24 months; and

         (ii) is temporarily unavailable to conduct the evaluation of the patient.

state, a medical practice act outlines the proper practice of medicine, including guidelines for writing prescriptions. Additionally, laws govern the actions of pharmacists and pharmacies. Passing laws usually takes time, and when online pharmacies first began popping up, some states were slow to respond. While some states already had laws requiring in-person examinations in order to write a prescription, other states' laws were not as clear.

For example, in Missouri, the medical practice act required a "sufficient examination" of patients in order for doctors to write a prescription when Dr. William Thompson began issuing prescriptions on the basis of an online questionnaire for a service called ePrescribe.[7] After a Connecticut law enforcement officer provided false information to obtain a weight-loss drug, Meridia, from Thompson, the state moved to discipline him. Thompson argued that he had, in fact, performed a "sufficient examination" each time he prescribed the weight loss drug because he collected information about each patient's height, weight, and blood pressure and asked for confirmation that the patient had had a recent medical exam. The medical board rejected Thompson's argument, holding:

> Thompson relied on his patient to tell him the truth on the questionnaire. He argues that all physicians rely to some extent on the patients to tell the truth about their medical histories. He also notes that a patient who lies to obtain a controlled substance is subject to criminal liability. There are two important factors, however, that would be confirmed by a visual or "in person" examination. The physician would see the body type of the patient, and a professional would take the patient's blood pressure.[8]

Acknowledging that online prescribing is a developing technology, the board stopped short of ruling that a physician could never prescribe medications without an in-person exam:

Considering all of the circumstances of this case and the arguments presented, we determine that Thompson did not perform a sufficient examination before prescribing Meridia, a controlled substance. This decision does not limit the concept of a sufficient examination to a face-to-face contact in every situation. However, we believe that the word "examination" . . . requires more than a questionnaire. Whether the doctor is seeing or otherwise examining the patient through the use of video conferencing or is otherwise examining the patient by touch, there must be some examination.[9]

While state legislatures have gradually been updating medical practice acts to limit online prescribing, state medical boards have generally frowned upon the practice even in the absence of a specific law, and the Federation of State Medical Boards has gone so far as to establish the National Clearinghouse on Internet Prescribing. This initiative includes a newsletter and action alerts that let each state's medical board know when a physician has been disciplined for writing a prescription in violation of a state's medical practice act. Therefore, if a physician is disciplined in one state, he or she risks having his license to practice terminated or suspended in other states in which he or she is licensed. Additionally, the physician will have difficulty obtaining a license to practice in additional states.

Many observers have suggested that the government's efforts to prevent online prescribing through questionnaires are simply overreaching by a government that already interferes too much with citizens' private lives. In the early days of online drug sales, libertarian political commentator Virginia Postrel blasted Missouri law enforcement officials for going after a Texas-based Internet pharmacy that had developed online questionnaires to sell drugs such as Propecia, allergy medication Claritin (which required a prescription at the time), and weight-loss drug Xenical. In her article, Postrel detailed how Missouri investigators lied on online questionnaires in order to obtain medications: "A pregnant assistant attorney general said she was a man and requested Propecia, [which] can cause birth defects if handled by a pregnant woman. In another case, an investigator said she was a man and ordered Viagra."[10] In Postrel's opinion, the government was overstepping its role as guardian of public safety: "States rely on stings to bring charges against online pharmacies because consumers haven't themselves complained. Unlike many regulatory actions, these aren't driven by public outcry or high-profile tragedies. There is no public demand for a crackdown."[11]

While some states have not cracked down on online prescribing, one state has actually moved to clarify situations in which online prescribing is permissible. Utah regulators, after pursuing action against an online pharmacy called KwikMed, ultimately entered into a consent agreement specifying the types of medications and the circumstances under which KwikMed's physicians could issue a prescription without physically examining the patient. Acting with the state's blessing, KwikMed developed detailed questionnaires for evaluating whether a patient can benefit from and safely take three specific erectile-dysfunction drugs, a hair-loss remedy, and a smoking-cessation aid at the same time.

An evaluation of KwikMed's legal online prescriptions was published in the journal of the prestigious Mayo Clinic. The study compared erectile dysfunction prescriptions for 500 of KwikMed's patients with 500 patients in traditional medical practices. The study found that there were no more inappropriate prescriptions among KwikMed patients than for patients of traditional clinics. Additionally, KwikMed scored higher on several measures of patient safety, while in traditional practices, important diagnostic questions included in KwikMed's questionnaire were often omitted from the in-person patient evaluation. The study by the University of Utah's Mark Munger and several collaborators determined that KwikMed was no better or worse than traditional medical clinics at prescribing erectile-dysfunction drugs:

> The e-medicine system demonstrated noninferiority to the traditional medicine system in the number of contraindicated prescriptions for PDE-5 inhibitors but was not superior. Prescription counseling occurred more often in the e-medicine system. The e-medicine system more frequently evaluated erectile dysfunction symptoms.[12]

In fact, the reason the online questionnaire might have produced similar results is that doctors often write prescriptions without doing a physical exam, even if medical standards require them. Doctors often write prescriptions for established patients without an office visit—for example, calling in antibiotics for a young patient who gets frequent ear infections. One lawyer noted that it was difficult to find doctors willing to testify on behalf of physicians who face discipline for online prescribing "because no doctor would step up and testify to what everyone knows: that conscientious physicians can and do sometimes issue prescriptions based solely on the sort of information that online questionnaires provide."[13]

Consumers should be protected from fraudulent or illegally imported medications.

Although the Ryan Haight Act was passed in 2008, Americans continue to receive spam e-mails touting the availability of OxyContin, Xanax, and other controlled substances without a prescription. A quick search reveals dozens of sites offering these drugs, as well as prescription drugs that are not controlled substances, such as Viagra. While federal law prohibits the dispensing of controlled substances in such a manner, and while state laws limit most other online prescribing, these drugs are nevertheless widely available. Most of the sites that offer such drugs are simply located outside of the United States and therefore out of the reach of state and federal authorities.

Peter Ax, a former investment banker who owns KwikMed, believes that while many states oppose their physicians writing prescriptions based on online questionnaires, this practice is much safer than allowing consumers to easily purchase medications from questionable overseas sources. KwikMed has widely publicized the results of Munger's study, which concluded:

> Results of the current study suggest that, under a platform of regulatory oversight, the safety of e-medicine care can match or possibly exceed traditional medical care, providing an evidence-based framework to reexamine current guidelines. . . . We recommend that state regulatory agencies consider the regulatory model of oversight protections implemented by the state of Utah to license Internet prescribing companies.[14]

In fact, KwikMed's Ax says he welcomes government efforts to crack down on "rogue" online pharmacies, telling the *New York Times*, "if we do things right, the bad guys who are less than ethical will go away, and our business will increase."[15] In other words, while state medical and pharmacy boards might not be comfortable with doctors writing prescriptions based on online questionnaires and pharmacists filling these prescriptions, at least if these actions are legal, the states and the federal government can regulate them. Egan warned Congress:

> There are pharmacies that are run by licensed pharmacists and there are doctors who are licensed doctors reviewing these questionnaires, and they are not being paid more to grant every single [prescription]. They are being paid by the review. If you have that in place, you have licensing authorities who can exercise control over these people. But if you criminalize that behavior, that particular

section of the industry will disappear, and, instead, what you will have is only offshore pharmacies.[16]

When people purchase drugs from a site that does not employ U.S. doctors or pharmacists, they are likely to get drugs from places such as China, India, Russia, Brazil, Pakistan, and Mexico—nations with less stringent oversight. While the government has stepped up enforcement efforts, the Ryan Haight Act and various state laws have not stopped people from obtaining prescription drugs without seeing a doctor in person. Instead, they might receive drugs that are counterfeit, expired, or mislabeled. None of the drugs imported from these countries is subjected to the quality controls to which drugs legally sold in the United States are.

In 2004, the U.S. Government Accountability Office conducted an investigation in which it attempted to purchase prescription drugs without a prior prescription from U.S., Canadian, and other foreign pharmacies. While some of the U.S. and Canadian pharmacies dispensed drugs without a prior prescription, they generally dispensed drugs otherwise in accordance with standard pharmacy practices, such as including information about side effects and shipping the drugs with a cold pack if necessary. In contrast, the drugs purchased from other foreign countries such as Mexico, Pakistan, and Turkey had a number of problems:

> None of the 21 samples from other foreign pharmacies included dispensing pharmacy labels that provided instructions for use, and only about one-third included warning information. Thirteen of the 21 samples displayed other problems associated with the handling of the drugs. For example, 3 samples of a drug that should be shipped in a temperature-controlled environment arrived in envelopes without insulation, and 5 samples contained tablets enclosed in punctured blister packs,

potentially exposing the tablets to damaging light or moisture. Finally, manufacturers reported that most of the drug samples from other foreign pharmacies (19 of 21 samples) were unapproved for the U.S. market because, for example, the labeling or the facilities in which they were manufactured had not been approved by FDA; however, they reported that the chemical composition of all but 4 of the other foreign samples was comparable to the product we had ordered. Among the 4 exceptions, 2 samples were found to be counterfeit versions of the product we had ordered, containing a lesser amount of the active ingredient, and 2 samples had a significantly different chemical composition than that of the product we had ordered.[17]

Summary

The federal government bans the sale of certain prescription drugs (called controlled substances) without a prescription issued by a doctor who has seen the patient in person. Many states prohibit doctors from writing prescriptions based solely on online questionnaires. Some evidence, however, suggests that online pharmacies employing licensed physicians and pharmacists might be as safe as traditional visits to doctors and pharmacies. Proponents of legalizing such online pharmacies say that carefully regulated online pharmacies will protect consumers, who otherwise would turn to "rogue" pharmacies located outside of the United States that sell counterfeit, expired, or mislabeled medicine.

Public Safety Demands Stronger Regulation of Online Pharmacies

O n February 11, 2001, Ryan Haight ate dinner with his mother after getting home from his part-time job. The California teen, who played varsity tennis and regularly earned straight A's in high school, had a bright future ahead of him. Before going to bed, he said, "I love you, Mom." Those were the last words Francine Haight would ever hear her son say. The next morning, she found her son in bed, unresponsive. Although she tried to resuscitate him, it was too late. He had died from an overdose of the prescription painkiller Vicodin, and his parents later found his stash of morphine and Valium, two other controlled substances.

Ryan's parents had given him a credit card to buy baseball cards on the Internet, but it turns out that Ryan was using the Internet to buy more than just baseball cards: He was buying the drugs that ultimately killed him. Speaking to a Senate committee, Mrs. Haight described her shock and anger that her son was able to purchase addictive and dangerous drugs when he was only 17:

> Ryan had made up a story. He had said he was 21. He said he had been in a car accident and had back pain, and he made up a doctor's name, Dr. Thomas, which happened to be his middle name. Dr. Robert Ogle, whom Ryan never saw and was never examined by, prescribed them, and an Internet pharmacy, Clayton Fuchs of Mainstreet Pharmacy, delivered them to our home. I was in shock. I thought, How could this be possible? I am a registered nurse; Ryan's father is a physician. We know that all controlled substances have to be accounted for. We count each and every drug that we give when we administer it to a patient. They are under lock and key. How could he get these off the Internet so easily? At a time when we were worried about our children being exposed to pornography and predators, marijuana and alcohol, we did not know that drug dealers were in our own family room.[1]

After taking some time to grieve privately, Mrs. Haight decided that she needed to use Ryan's story to help prevent similar tragedies. Ultimately, the federal law that banned prescribing controlled substances over the Internet without an in-person examination bore Ryan Haight's name. Yet, while Mrs. Haight and her supporters won a victory, the war against online prescribing is far from over. Earlier versions of the law had called for a ban on *any* types of prescriptions being issued over the Internet without an in-person exam, not just the more highly regulated category of controlled substances. Opponents of this practice say that it is unsafe to write prescriptions for someone a doctor has never met, and many state medical boards agree. While they welcome vigorous

Francine Haight with photos of her son Ryan, a California teen-ager who died from an overdose of the prescription painkiller Vicodin, which he had purchased illegally over the Internet in 2001.

enforcement of the Ryan Haight Act, they also would like the nationwide ban extended to every prescription drug, curtailing sales of popular drugs such as the erectile-dysfunction drug Viagra. Critics of online prescribing say that offshore pharmacies that ignore U.S. laws are a separate problem and should not be used as an excuse to loosen restrictions of U.S. doctors and pharmacists.

An online questionnaire is not a safe basis for writing a prescription.

As previously mentioned, when he purchased controlled substances on the Internet, Ryan Haight was 17 but told the prescribing physician he was 21. Arguably, he might have gotten away with this lie if he had seen a doctor in person. He might have even been able to convince a doctor that he had chronic pain, although many doctors would want to at least see his medical records pertaining to his supposed car accident. Over the Internet, however, he never had to look anyone in the eye, and it was simple to get away with his lies.

The inability to screen out drug-seeking behavior, however, is not the only risk associated with online prescribing. There are many considerations that doctors must weigh when writing prescriptions, and it is difficult to evaluate them without having ever seen a patient in person. Some of the risks associated with substituting online questionnaires for the traditional doctor-patient relationship include: missed diagnoses, inappropriate prescriptions, side effects, and drug interactions.

When patients obtain prescription drugs over the Internet instead of by visiting a doctor, there is a great risk that serious conditions will be undiagnosed or misdiagnosed. Like Ryan Haight, John McKay was a young Californian with a bright future. As a freshman at Stanford University, McKay was suffering from serious depression and had suicidal thoughts. He confided these suicidal urges to a friend, but he did not confide them to Dr. Christian Hageseth, a physician who reviewed an online questionnaire that McKay filled out in order to purchase fluoxetine, an antidepressant sold under the brand name Prozac. Instead, McKay indicated that he suffered from "moderate depression and major attention deficit."[2] On August 2, 2005, McKay's mother and brother arrived at the family home and found him in his car with the engine running, a garden hose running from the tailpipe into the passenger compartment. They broke into the car and tried to revive him, but McKay had succumbed to carbon monoxide poisoning.

Like Haight's death, McKay's death might in the long run help to save others' lives. Although a federal court ruled that the fluoxetine did not contribute to the suicide, the state of California took action against Hageseth for practicing medicine in the state without a license. Ultimately, Hageseth chose not to continue fighting the charges and accepted a deal with prosecutors involving jail time. After taking the deal, he spoke out about the case, arguing that people need access to antidepressants but acknowledging that Internet prescribing is not the answer. Instead, he started Depression Care Access, a nonprofit organization. Its mission is to provide people who cannot afford psychiatric care with financial assistance to have two in-person consultations with a doctor.[3]

Online questionnaires that can be taken quickly and anonymously do have some usefulness in the practice of medicine, but they should be thought of as a screening tool that helps people decide whether they might need to see a doctor. Online questionnaires should not be substituted for a doctor's visit because medications might end up being used to treat the symptoms of a serious underlying condition. Dr. James Winn of the Federation of State Medical Boards warned men not to use an online pharmacy to obtain a prescription for Viagra or other erectile-dysfunction drugs. He said, "Erectile dysfunction is not a disease; it's a symptom. It may occur because of multiple problems, including depression, diabetes, vascular problems or a pituitary tumor. It's the physician's responsibility to sort that out, and to determine the treat-ment."[4] In other words, consumers can generally tell when they have a symptom, but most people lack an understanding of what causes the symptom. The Medical Board of California's Department of Consumer Affairs warns: "Self-diagnosing can be dangerous, and treating a symptom without determining the underlying cause may mask symptoms that will prevent appropriate treatment of a serious, and maybe life-threaten-ing, disease or condition."[5] By simply treating the symptom by purchasing a medication online, a serious disease might go undetected or worsen.

In their efforts to rein in online pharmacies, various state investigators have been able to purchase inappropriate prescriptions by providing false information. Much as Ryan Haight was able to conceal his true identity easily on the online questionnaire, state investigators have easily obtained medica-tions that were inappropriate for the people who ultimately received them. A Connecticut investigator, for example, was able to obtain a prescription from a Missouri doctor for a weight-loss drug even though the investigator was not suf-ficiently overweight to meet the prescribing guidelines for the drug. A pregnant prosecutor from Missouri was able to obtain a prescription for Propecia, a hair-loss remedy, even though the drug causes severe birth defects and should not even be handled by a pregnant woman.

Even consumers who fill out online questionnaires to the best of their knowledge are putting themselves at risk of side effects if they purchase medications online. The Medical Board of California warns:

> All drugs, particularly prescription drugs, have the potential for dangerous side effects. After the pre-scription is sold, it is likely that the prescribing online physician will not be available to help you. Patients need a physician with whom they have a relationship

to monitor and treat their conditions for a number of very good reasons. In the event of side effects, if the condition worsens, or if there is an interaction with other drugs, each patient needs a physician who is aware of his or her condition and the medications.[6]

An additional problem is that some prescription medications cannot be taken safely with certain other prescription or nonprescription medications. For example, every Viagra

THE LETTER OF THE LAW

State Laws and Policies Against Online Prescribing

An increasing number of states have either banned or condemned online prescribing. In general, a state's legislature must pass a law to create criminal or civil penalties for online prescribing. A number of state medical boards, which administer the practice of medicine, have also condemned the practice.

Kentucky Revised Statutes, Section 311.597

"[D]ishonorable, unethical, or unprofessional conduct of a character likely to deceive, defraud, or harm the public or any member thereof "shall include . . . prescrib[ing] or dispens[ing] any medication . . . in response to any communication transmitted or received by computer or other electronic means, when the licensee fails to take the following actions to establish and maintain a proper physician-patient relationship:

1. Verification that the person requesting medication is in fact who the patient claims to be;

2. Establishment of a documented diagnosis through the use of accepted medical practices; and

3. Maintenance of a current medical record.

For the purposes of this paragraph, an electronic, online, or telephonic evaluation by questionnaire is inadequate for the initial evaluation of the patient or for any follow-up evaluation.

television commercial contains a disclaimer that the medication cannot be taken by someone who is taking nitrate heart medications because the combination of the drugs can cause an unsafe drop in blood pressure. In an investigation of online pharmacies, the FDA tested whether the pharmacies would detect potential drug interactions. The investigator was able to submit a purchase order for the cholesterol-lowering drug Lipitor even after claiming to be taking the antibiotic erythromycin—two drugs that should not be taken together.

**Alabama Administrative Code 540-X-9-.11,
Contact With Patients Before Prescribing**

(1) It is the position of the Board that prescribing drugs to an individual the prescriber has not personally examined is usually inappropriate. Before prescribing a drug, a physician should make an informed medical judgment based on the circumstances of the situation and on his or her training and experience. Ordinarily, this will require that the physician personally perform an appropriate history and physical examination, make a diagnosis, and formulate a therapeutic plan, a part of which might be a prescription. This process must be documented appropriately.

(2) Prescribing for a patient whom the physician has not personally examined may be suitable under certain circumstances. These may include, but not be limited to, admission orders for a patient newly admitted to a health care facility, prescribing for a patient of another physician for whom the prescriber is taking call, or continuing medication on a short-term basis for a new patient prior to the patient's first appointment. Established patients may not require a new history and physical examination for each new prescription, depending on good medical practice.

(3) It is the position of the Board that prescribing drugs to individuals the physician has never met based solely on answers to a set of questions, as is common in Internet or toll-free telephone prescribing, is inappropriate and unprofessional.

The Ryan Haight Act of 2008 was necessary to prevent tragedies such as Ryan Haight's death. While state medical boards oppose all forms of online prescribing and have vigorously supported legislation that would ban it, the version of the Ryan Haight Act that was signed into law prohibited online prescribing only of controlled substances, such as painkillers and stimulants. These drugs have legitimate medical uses, but they also have a great potential for abuse. Many are extremely addictive. The federal government has launched ongoing public awareness campaigns warning parents that teens frequently take controlled substances from their parents' medicine cabinets in order to get high or sell them for cash. Purchasing them on the Internet, however, is another way that teens such as Ryan Haight, as well as adult drug users and even drug dealers, have obtained controlled substances easily.

Testifying during a congressional hearing about the Ryan Haight Act, Drug Enforcement Administration (DEA) official Joseph Rannazzisi warned lawmakers that while there are many ways for people to get prescription drugs for nonmedical purposes (e.g., to get "high"), the involvement of licensed doctors and licensed pharmacists played a major role in getting these drugs from the manufacturers onto the street. He pointed out that just a few of the worst offenders put a lot more OxyContin into the hands of abusers than could possibly be taken from people's medicine cabinets:

In 2006, DEA identified 34 known or suspected rogue Internet pharmacies that dispensed over 98 million dosage units of hydrocodone-combination products. To put this into perspective, the average legitimate pharmacy in the U.S. dispenses approximately 88,000 dosage units of hydrocodone-combo products per year. DEA investigations of these Internet traffickers have found that the vast majority are linked to DEA-registered pharmacies and DEA-registered doctors.[7]

Even with the Ryan Haight Act in place, addicts and drug abusers find a way to get OxyContin and other controlled substances. The law, however, takes a major step toward reducing the supply while still allowing those with a legitimate prescription the opportunity to shop for the best price on the Internet.

Legitimate telemedicine offers convenience and cost savings without the risks of online pharmacies. Operators of online pharmacies, even though they run for-profit businesses, often claim they provide a valuable public service to people who are unable to get to a doctor's office for an appointment or cannot afford traditional medical care. Think of a person with limited means living in, for example, a remote Alaskan village. During the winter, obtaining medical care might indeed be difficult. The cost of transportation, added to the cost of a doctor's visit, might make it impossible to pay for care.

Over the past decade the practice of "telemedicine" has greatly expanded, with the support of federal government programs such as the Veterans Health Administration and Medicare, the latter of which serves disabled and older Americans. Physicians and other professionals who practice telemedicine use technology such as the Internet, video conferencing, and even traditional telephone service to communicate with patients in other locations. Telemedicine also includes communication among health care professionals; for example, a doctor might consult with a cancer specialist by transmitting test results electronically to the specialist. Telemedicine has obvious benefits for people living in frontier and rural communities, such as remote Alaskan villages. In fact, the state of Alaska has supported several telemedicine initiatives. The goal, however, is not to evade the traditional doctor-patient relationship in order to obtain prescription drugs. Instead, mechanisms are set up for the rural patient to establish a doctor-patient relationship and then communicate when necessary. For example, in some small communities, the drugstore or senior center might set up video conferencing facilities so that people can communicate with a physician. In areas with a shortage of physicians, a traveling nurse might perform routine screenings and then communicate the results to a physician electronically.

Telemedicine is also beneficial to people with chronic diseases, even if they live close to their doctors' offices, because it allows them to manage their condition more effectively without the expense and inconvenience of a doctor's visit. For example, a person who has diabetes can upload a month's worth of blood glucose readings to an endocrinologist, who can evaluate the results to determine whether to change dosages of insulin or other medications. New technologies support remote monitoring of heart patients as well.

During the debates over the Ryan Haight Act, the Federation of State Medical Boards emphasized the importance (and difficulty) of distinguishing between the legitimate practice of telemedicine and practices that put profits over patient safety:

> The appropriate application of technology can enhance medical care by improving patient access to specialty care, facilitating communication with physicians and other health care providers, filling prescriptions, obtaining laboratory results, scheduling appointments, monitoring chronic conditions, providing health care information, and clarifying medical advice. At the same time, new technologies can create opportunities for individuals and entities to exploit technological advancements for personal gain without regard for patient safety. The simultaneous increase in telemedicine technologies/applications and "rogue" Internet pharmacies, those that prescribe and dispense medication based on online consultations or questionnaires, have created complex regulatory challenges for state medical boards in protecting the public.[8]

Recognizing that the needs of Americans in rural and frontier areas and with chronic conditions are served by telemedicine, Congress included a number of telemedicine exceptions to the general rule against online prescribing. For example, a remote physician may issue a prescription to a person who is physically present in a hospital or health clinic. Additionally, provisions in the law allow for the issuing of prescriptions online by physicians practicing under special arrangements with the Indian Health Service.

Outlawing online prescribing does not promote offshore pharmacies.

Those who want to legalize online prescribing say that allowing U.S. doctors to write prescriptions on the basis of an online questionnaire and allowing U.S. pharmacists to fill these

New York State Board for Professional Medical Conduct, Statements on Telemedicine, December 24, 2003

The practice of telemedicine can be characterized as follows:

- The geographic separation between two or more participants and/or entities engaged in health care,

- The use of telecommunication and related technology to gather, store and disseminate health-related information, and

- The use of electronic interactive technologies to assess, diagnose and/or treat medical conditions.

All the current standards of care regarding the practice of medicine apply. The fact that an electronic medium is utilized for contact between parties or as a substitute for face-to-face consultation does not change the standards of care.

Source: http://www.health.state.ny.us/nysdoh/opmc/telemedicine.htm.

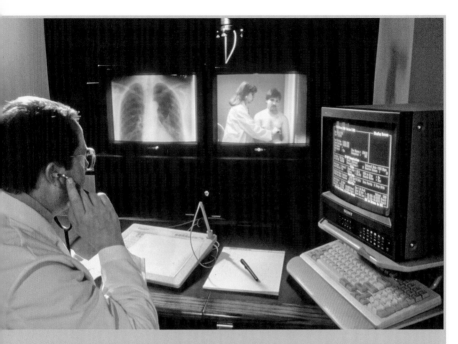

Telemedicine—in which medical information is transferred via the Internet for the purpose of consulting—is a rapidly developing aspect of medicine. Today, many doctors conduct medical examinations or procedures remotely.

prescriptions is much safer than the alternative. If consumers are unable to purchase drugs from sites that involve U.S. doctors and pharmacists, the argument goes, consumers will instead go to "rogue" sites illegally selling counterfeit, mislabeled, or improperly handled medications from overseas that have not been subject to any medical review.

Critics of online pharmacies, however, say that consumers deserve safe access to prescription drugs, not just the "less unsafe" access offered when U.S. physicians prescribe on the basis of online questionnaires. Banning *all* online prescribing would allow the government to put out consistent warnings to consumers that they should never purchase medication online unless they have been to a doctor and gotten a prescription for that medication. Additionally, critics of online prescribing say that it is easier to put on a unified front against all pharmacies that sell prescription medications without a prior prescription. Large pharmacy chains, such as Walgreens and CVS, do not hawk prescription medications online, nor do legitimate independent pharmacies. Instead, they offer an affordable means of purchasing medications that a licensed physician has prescribed within the traditional doctor-patient relationship.

The National Association of Boards of Pharmacy, a group representing state pharmacy licensing boards, has established the Verified Internet Pharmacy Practice Sites (VIPPS) program to identify pharmacies that abide by all laws and professional standards. They ship prescription drugs to people who have prescriptions and do not help people get prescriptions of questionable validity using an online questionnaire. VIPPS, however, is a voluntary program, and therefore it is difficult for law enforcement officials to limit access to other Internet pharmacies. Critics of online prescribing would like a law allowing the DEA or the FDA to maintain this list. As Christine Jones of GoDaddy.com—one of the services that provides the URLs that allow people to access Web sites by name—told Congress, the lack of a certified list of legitimate online pharmacies makes it hard for GoDaddy and other domain name registrars to block access to rogue online pharmacies:

> But today there is nothing that makes the content per se illegal. So, like, for example, with child pornography, the National Center for Missing and Exploited Children or the FBI or ICE or another agency can come to us and say, "We know that there is a child pornography site operating on your network; could you please take it down?" and we say, "Absolutely." No questions, no notice, "You go away, because what you are doing is illegal."

That is the kind of tool that we are looking for with the online pharmacy sites, not to disable the valid 2,000 sites in Ohio, but to disable the invalid, counterfeit, no-prescription-needed Web sites. If we had that tool, then we could just say, "Are you on the list? If you are not on the list, you have to go away until you get your name on the list. It doesn't matter to me where you are. You can be overseas, you can be in any State, could be on the moon, I don't care. Get your name on the list, or you have to go away."[9]

Summary
While the Internet has the potential to improve health care access while reducing costs to consumers, some safeguards are important. Critics of online pharmacies would like online pre-scribing limited to patients actually examined by a doctor or in the context of legitimate telemedicine, in which the patient is present at some sort of health center and the doctor has access to the patient's full medical record. Banning online prescribing and or creating a certification process for pharmacies would help local, state, and federal officials recognize "pharmacies" that are really outlets for illegal and improper sales of prescription drugs.

Restrictions on Social Networking Will Hamper a Valuable Communications Tool

The 2008 presidential election was historic in many ways. The Democrats had nominated a black candidate, Senator Barack Obama, for president, and Republican candidate Senator John McCain had picked a woman, Governor Sarah Palin, to be his vice-presidential running mate. Going into the general election, the public knew that for the first time, someone other than a white male would serve as either president or vice president. It was also the first time that online social networks were used extensively by the candidates. Social-networking sites such as MySpace, Facebook, and Twitter allow people to build so-called "online communities"—networks of friends, followers, or fans—who can be contacted instantly, and who can in turn contact their friends, fans, or followers instantly. For example, when a candidate gave a rousing speech, supporters could send a link to their network members, some of whom would send it to their network, and so on. The same was done by opponents of a candidate when he or she said or did something objectionable. This type of messaging to an increasing numbers of people is sometimes described as "viral" because of the way it spreads from person to person.

During the primary season and general elections, all of the candidates' campaigns used social networking to some extent, and supporters of various candidates used Facebook, MySpace, Twitter, and other services to build support for the candidate of their choice. No candidate, however, used social networking as effectively as Obama did. His use of social networking was a key factor in his winning the presidency. In fact, his campaign brought on Chris Hughes, co-founder of Facebook, to create MyBarackObama.com. The site, which operated like other social-networking sites, allowed users to create a profile proclaiming support for Obama the candidate, form local groups of supporters, plan local events, raise money for the campaign, and persuade undecided or ambivalent voters. According to *Fast Company*, "By the time the campaign was over, volunteers had created more than 2 million profiles on the site, planned 200,000 offline events, formed 35,000 groups, posted 400,000 blogs, and raised $30 million on 70,000 personal fund-raising pages."[1]

Social-networking sites also have a dark side, however. Cases in which adults have lured teens into a sexual relationship or those in which people have harassed or threatened emotionally vulnerable adolescents have grabbed headlines. An example of the latter occurred when the federal government prosecuted a Missouri woman for computer fraud in 2008 for using a fake online profile of a teenage boy on MySpace in order to play with the heartstrings of one of her daughter's rivals. The rival 13-year-old girl hanged herself after receiving a message from the imaginary boy stating that "[t]he world would be a better place without you."[2] Although such cases are extremely rare among social-networking sites' millions of users, they generate a strong emotional response from the public. As a result, local, state, and federal officials have tried to keep convicted sex offenders off of the sites and have also sought to limit teens' access to social-networking sites. For example, many school systems and public libraries do not allow their computers to be used to access popular social-networking sites.

Critics say that such restrictions are shortsighted. While objectionable uses of social networking get most of the attention, the example set by Obama's campaign shows the power to bring people together to support a cause, form friendships, and debate issues important to the nation's future. While some users might be susceptible to improper contact from others, parents and schools can educate young people about ways to protect themselves. The major sites devote significant resources to keeping improper activity off their networks, and supporters of an unrestricted Internet say that these efforts, when combined with education of young people, is sufficient, and that legal restrictions are unwarranted.

Social-networking sites promote creativity, friendship, and even democracy.

Throughout the United States, school districts have established policies prohibiting access to social-networking sites, such as MySpace and Facebook, from school computers. Although the schools use "filtering" software that blocks access to the sites, students consistently find ways to get around the technology, and schools therefore must discipline students for violating their policies. Many schools also subject students to discipline for material that they post on these sites or on personal Web sites, even if the material was created outside of school. Examples of acts subjected to discipline include "cyberbullying" (making threats to other students), sexually explicit material, and material critical of teachers or school administrators. One Catholic school in a Detroit suburb went so far as to announce a policy that no student who had a MySpace profile would be allowed to attend school. (The school has kindergarten through eighth grade; MySpace policy prohibits anyone under 14 from joining.)

An even more interesting debate has been going on in the world of public libraries. On the one hand, libraries have established profiles on MySpace and Facebook so that they can communicate with patrons and publicize library events and resources. On the other hand, a large number of public libraries have begun to use filtering software to block access to social-networking sites. The typical rationales are that patrons might view objectionable content such as pornography and that young people might be exposed to sexual predators. Even though the sites have specific policies regarding objectionable content, these policies rely on taking down content that is reported, rather than clearing content in advance. Therefore, some amount of objectionable content might be posted at any given time.

Blanket bans on social networking, however, ignore the many important and educational uses of the sites. In addition to politicians using them successfully, the sites have the potential for helping more young people care about political issues and motivating them to vote when they turn 18. Additionally, the sites offer a means of raising awareness and raising money for social concerns. For example, a Connecticut teen whose grandmother had been diagnosed with Parkinson's disease used Facebook to help raise money for research and to get a fundraising walk off the ground.

The "viral" nature of social-networking sites means that people can start small and achieve big results. Two high school classmates, Ana Slavin and Nick Anderson, were gravely concerned about events in Darfur, a region in the African nation Sudan. Hundreds of thousands of people have been killed in ongoing violence, and the international community has condemned the violence and the Sudanese government's response. In order to raise awareness of the problem among students, Slavin and Anderson started Dollars for Darfur. The campaign, which is aimed at teens, uses online networking sites to promote its mission. Slavin told a congressional committee examining Darfur:

> As Nick and I were developing Dollars for Darfur, there was one aspect that was of primary importance: the involvement of high school students. While some view high school students to be concerned with merely the trials and tribulations of teenage life, we saw something more. We saw a generation with the desire to make a difference.
>
> Our generation has struggled to find an identity. We are now recognized for our activism. Through this challenge we have proved that, given the right forum, we can have an impact.
>
> Nick and I started Dollars for Darfur by simply inviting our friends to join our Facebook and MySpace groups and encouraging them to spread the word. The numbers grew exponentially. In just 6 months, more than 7,000 high school students had joined our groups.[3]

Slavin and Anderson were called to testify before Congress in large part because of the attention that the social-networking sites helped them gain for their cause. With hundreds of Facebook "friends," they not only raised more than $300,000, but they ended up appearing on national television and jointly were named ABC News Person of the Week.

For some people, the benefit of MySpace and similar sites might simply be the encouragement of self-expression. One young blogger wrote, "Many teens post their unique poetry and display their own art on their profile. . . . MySpace also boosts shy people's self esteem. Some teens even allege that MySpace has changed their social life completely. Whatever the case may be, MySpace has a positive effect on teens."[4]

The risks to children have been distorted and overstated.

Efforts to "protect teens" are often a safe bet for politicians to win points with the electorate, as many of the people who are affected when the laws go too far are too young to vote. Teens and young adults adopted the technology of social networking much more quickly than did their parents, so making social networking a target of legislation had an added appeal because it was an attack upon something seen by many as an unwanted advancement in technology.

The U.S. House of Representatives held hearings in 2006 that focused on dealing with the problem of adults initiating sexual relationships with minors through the Internet. Findings suggested that one in five children had been sexually solicited online. Expert after expert testified as to the dangers of MySpace, which was referred to in one hearing as a "virtual Sears catalog for pedophiles."[5] As a result of the hearings, the House voted 410 to 15 to pass a bill referred to as the Deleting Online Predators Act of 2006 (DOPA). The bill would have required that libraries and schools restrict access to social-networking sites. At the time of the House's passage, the president of the American Library Association said:

> This unnecessary and overly broad legislation will hinder students' ability to engage in distance learning and block library computer users from accessing a wide array of essential Internet applications including instant messaging, email, wikis and blogs.
>
> Under DOPA, people who use library and school computers as their primary conduits to the Internet will be unfairly blocked from accessing some of the web's most powerful emerging technologies and learning applications.[6]

Despite overwhelming support for DOPA in the House of Representatives, experts who have studied the issue object to the way the problem is being presented. Without specifically opposing the law, the Crimes Against Children Research Center at the University of New Hampshire, which published a 2005 study on the topic, issued a clarification of statistics relating to online sexual solicitations. One problem the researchers pointed out was that supporters of restrictions tend to lump all types of sexually suggestive communications together, such as a lewd comment inquiring about a classmate's bra size, to make the problem seem more significant. Another problem is that supporters of restrictions tend to characterize all solicitations as being from "predators," when in fact many of the communications come from other youths, including those known personally by the recipient.

In sum, the University of New Hampshire study detected little actual danger to children. In their nationwide study, only two children reported being sexually assaulted, which is too small a number to extrapolate to a percentage. The researchers suggested the following as a more accurate portrayal of their findings:

- 1 in 25 youth (about 4%) got "aggressive" sexual solicitations that included attempts to contact the youth offline. These are the episodes most likely to result in actual victimizations. (About one-quarter of these aggressive solicitations came from people the youth knew in person, mostly other youth.)
- 1 in 25 youth (about 4%) were solicited to take sexual pictures of themselves. . . .
- 1 in 25 youth (about 4%) said they were upset or distressed as a result of an online solicitation.[7]

Most often, the researchers reported, the youths were not frightened or intimidated by the communications and responded by blocking or warning the solicitors.

Additionally, legislators seemed to have focused on social-networking sites because they represented a new, poorly understood technology, rather than because they were more dangerous than other types of Internet communication. In an article published in the medical journal *Pediatrics,* two of the same researchers noted:

> Based on national data from 1588 youth between the ages of 10 and 15 years, our findings suggest that online interpersonal victimizations do not seem to occur to any greater degree and, in fact, seem to occur to a lesser degree in social networking sites than other places online where youth communicate with others. . . . Findings suggest that targeting social networking sites specifically may not be the best method of reducing the prevalence of online interpersonal victimization of children and younger adolescents. . . . Our findings suggest that 15% of all youth report being targeted by unwanted sexual solicitation, 4% in a social networking site specifically.[8]

While DOPA never became law, Congress did eventually pass the Keeping the Internet Devoid of Sexual Predators Act of 2008, also referred to by its partial acronym, the "KIDS Act of 2008."[9] The KIDS Act requires sex offenders to report any online identifiers, such as e-mail addresses or screen names, to state sex offender registries. The law also requires the U.S. Department of Justice to maintain a secure database of these online identifiers so that social-networking sites can compare their user information to the sex offender data and identify any sex offenders using the site. The law stopped short of requiring social-networking sites to use the database.

Of course, once the database was in place, it would have been a public relations nightmare for Facebook and MySpace not to use it and purge sex offenders from their sites. Additionally, some states have decided to take a more assertive approach than the federal government did. The attorneys general of Connecticut and North Carolina demanded a list of registered sex offenders whom MySpace had booted. In February 2009, MySpace handed over a list of more than 90,000 banished sex offenders. Not all state attorneys general, however, support the idea that pursuing sex offenders who use MySpace and Facebook is a worthwhile use of resources. The momentum for state enforcement was set

Deleting Online Predators Act of 2006 (DOPA), H.R. 5319, 109th Congress, 2nd Session

Although the U.S. House of Representatives passed this bill, the Senate never voted on it, and it never became law. An excerpt is presented below:

(1) sexual predators approach minors on the Internet using chat rooms and social networking websites, and, according to the United States Attorney General, one in five children has been approached sexually on the Internet;

(2) sexual predators can use these chat rooms and websites to locate, learn about, befriend, and eventually prey on children by engaging them in sexually explicit conversations, asking for photographs, and attempting to lure children into a face to face meeting; and

(3) with the explosive growth of trendy chat rooms and social networking websites, it is becoming more and more difficult to monitor and protect minors from those with devious intentions, particularly when children are away from parental supervision.

The proposed law therefore required that any school receiving federal support for telecommunications or Internet must use software that:

Protects against access to a commercial social networking website or chat room unless used for an educational purpose with adult supervision.

Any library receiving this federal support must use software that:

Protects against access by minors without parental authorization to a commercial social networking website or chat room, and informs parents that sexual predators can use these websites and chat rooms to prey on children.

back by a task force formed by a working group of state attorneys general. According to the task force's report, some of the central premises of the case against social-networking sites are false. While the media and Congress focused on adult sex offenders pretending to be children so that they could lure young victims into encounters, this report, commissioned by Harvard University, found little evidence of such behavior. It concluded:

> Although identity deception may occur online, it does not appear to play a large role in criminal cases in which adult sex offenders have been arrested for sex crimes in which they met victims online. Interviews with police indicate that most victims are underage adolescents who know they are going to meet adults for sexual encounters and the offenses tended to fit a model of statutory rape involving a post-pubescent minor having nonforcible sexual relations with an adult, most frequently adults in their twenties.[10]

Parents and schools bear the responsibility for teaching online safety.

A major lesson to be learned from the Harvard report is that preventing sexual abuse of minors should focus on identifying people who are at risk rather than trying to interfere with a technology that poses risks for a small percentage of its users. Noting that the media "does not paint an accurate picture" of sexual abuse initiated online, the report concluded that the hysteria "leads to major risks in this area being ignored."[11] Rather than being tied to "any particular technological platform" the risk of sexual abuse "appears to be more correlated with a youth's psychosocial profile and risky behaviors."[12]

The Children's Internet Protection Act,[13] enacted in 2000, requires schools and libraries to establish Internet safety policies in order to receive federal support for Internet access. In 2008, Congress, in the Protecting Children in the 21st Century Act,[14] further defines the requirement for these policies, noting that "part of [an] Internet safety policy is educating minors about appropriate online behavior, including interacting with other individuals on social networking websites and in chat rooms and cyberbullying awareness and response."[15]

Online safety includes issues regarding the use of the Internet in a manner that promotes safe activity for children, protects children from cybercrimes, including crimes by online predators, and helps parents shield their children from material that is inappropriate for minors. Unfortunately, some experts say, the prevention education that is already taking place is misguided because it makes incorrect assumptions about young people and focuses on ineffective strategies. In an article published in *American Psychologist*, University of New Hampshire researchers noted that most teens, even younger teens, are aware of Internet technologies and sexual issues and are able to differentiate between safe and unsafe interactions. The authors lament the fact that prevention efforts focus so much on parents (who might not know what their children are doing online) and not enough on teens (who know what they are doing online). Noting that teens need "specific, age-appropriate information," the article suggests that teens need frank information explaining that adults who solicit them are breaking the law and that taking pictures with a "webcam" can result in the images being traded by child pornographers worldwide.[16]

Further, the article noted that existing prevention efforts focus on ineffective strategies such as not posting personal information online, even though research has shown that youths who post information about themselves or write blogs are no more susceptible to online sexual solicitations than other youths. The authors suggest that prevention education should focus on limiting behaviors that have been shown to increase risk, such as discussing sex with unknown people: "Overly broad admonishments about talking to strangers may be seen as unrealistic and undercut credibility."[17]

Social-networking sites cannot be expected to police all activity.

While social-networking sites have been targeted because of their popularity among young people, critics of regulating them point out that the very usefulness of the medium depends on inter-personal communication. The sheer volume of communication online makes it impossible to monitor all of it. Additionally, the major social-networking sites have taken reasonable steps to protect users, including terms of service that users must follow or risk having their membership restricted or terminated. Facebook, for example, sparked protests from women's groups beginning in late 2008 when it removed any pictures in which a woman's nipples were exposed, including photos of women breastfeeding their infants.

Chris Kelly, Facebook's chief privacy officer, testified before Congress about the steps the company takes to deter misuse of the network:

> We have a report this user, report this link, report this photo on every page in Facebook and our . . . customer service staff can easily process complaints. . . . They can launch an investigation and they often remove members who improperly get into a service. So we also empower our members to make choices in what they display on their site and to whom they display it. We have very detailed privacy settings and choices and we also use technological monitoring tools to look at possible indications of antisocial behavior on the site. If somebody were to . . . start to try to befriend too many people, try to reach out and get rejected friend requests, that is one of the things that we measure. It highlights a user account and allows us to investigate that.[18]

At the same hearing, Michael Angus, a MySpace official, discussed the site's procedures for protecting youths from inappropriate interactions. A cornerstone is the use of privacy controls that limit who can view young users' profiles. Angus said:

> Profiles of users who are 14 and 15 are automatically set to private. We also now require that all users over the age of 18 must either know the email address or the first and last name of a member who is 14 or 15 to invite that member to become their friend.... That allows our users to control the access and scope of their community.[19]

MySpace also uses a combination of technology and manpower to keep offensive content off its network. As of 2006, Angus reported:

Excerpt from Facebook's Statement of Rights and Responsibilities (revised May 1, 2009)

We do our best to keep Facebook safe, but we cannot guarantee it. We need your help in order to do that, which includes the following commitments ...

5. You will not bully, intimidate, or harass any user.
6. You will not post content that is hateful, threatening, pornographic, or that contains nudity or graphic or gratuitous violence....
8. You will not use Facebook to do anything unlawful, misleading, malicious, or discriminatory.

Facebook users provide their real names and information, and we need your help to keep it that way. Here are some commitments you make to us relating to registering and maintaining the security of your account ...

1. You will not provide any false personal information on Facebook, or create an account for anyone other than yourself without permission.
2. You will not use Facebook if you are under 13....
4. You will not use Facebook if you are a convicted sex offender.

Source: http://www.facebook.com/terms/english.php.

MySpace reviews over 3 million images uploaded daily for content that violate our terms of use and we immediately remove any images that violate these terms. We also provide a link with each hosted image to allow users to report inappropriate content.

We recently developed and implemented proprietary technology to screen images on MySpace to assist us in quickly eradicating images that do not meet our standards. We also now provide a direct link to the cyber tip line to allow users to report incidents of child exploitation directly to the National Center. In addition, each page of our site contains a link to allow users to report inappropriate content and any other abuses that may occur on the site.[20]

While monitoring every online conversation would be impossible, Angus reported that MySpace does attempt to keep minors away from areas of the site that are likely to cause trouble: "We have identified certain discussion groups that may contain material that is inappropriate for those under 18. Users under the age of 18 or who are not logged in cannot see or join these groups."[21]

Summary

Social-networking sites are enormously popular, particularly among young people. Tens of millions of people are using the sites to connect with friends, debate ideas, share photos, discuss musical artists, and many other legitimate purposes. Online sexual solicitations represent but a tiny fraction of the activities on these sites. While Congress and state attorneys general have tried to restrict the medium, critics say that focusing on prevention, particularly for those with identified high-risk behaviors, will be more effective and will not interfere with the valuable interactions of the vast majority of users.

Social Networks Are Accessible to Youths and Therefore Must Be Made Safe

In spring 2006, 19-year-old Matt, calling himself a new kid in town, started using MySpace to make friends in Middletown, Connecticut. A number of teenage girls, some 14 and 15, started becoming his online "friends"—once he appeared on these girls' friend lists, it was a lot easier to make new "friends" because these new friends saw that he was listed on their own friends' sites. Once Matt became "friends" with these girls, he was able to access a wide variety of personal information, including pictures, names, home and cell phone numbers, and even locations where they would be at certain times. One 16-year-old girl eventually suggested meeting Matt in person.

These girls should have known better than to share private information with someone whom they did not know personally. That same spring, more than a dozen girls under age 16 in the area had been sexually assaulted by adult males they met online. Fortunately for the young girls who befriended Matt, he was not an online predator. He also, however, was not a 19-year-old young man who was new in town. Instead, "Matt" was really Detective Frank Dannahey of the Rocky Hill, Connecticut, Police Department. He was trying to find out how difficult or easy it would be for a sexual predator to disguise his identity and meet underage girls. It turns out it was very easy.

Dannahey made arrangements with some of the girls' parents to have the girls interviewed by "Dateline NBC." Unaware of Matt's true identity, the girls were asked whether they revealed personal information online. They said they did not. They were then asked if they conversed online with people they did not know, and again they denied it. Soon afterward, Dannahey was introduced to the girls as "Matt." The girls were surprised, not only that Matt was actually an older police officer, but also that they had revealed as much information as they had to someone they did not know.

Usually, law enforcement officers go undercover on the other side of the online relationship—they pose as young boys or girls and wait for the sexual predators to come to them. Across the country, police are busy making up online identities and setting up meetings with unsuspecting predators who think they are meeting with a minor to have sex, only to be arrested. Critics of social-networking sites say that these sting operations should not be needed to the extent they are. They point to the fact that social-networking sites are generally operated as profit-making ventures, and with millions of members, they should be able to afford the best technology to protect young people who use the sites. While opponents of regulation say abuse of unsuspecting young children is rare, supporters say that even one incident of sexual abuse is too many. Many believe that parents have the primary responsibility to protect their children, but with rapidly changing technology, they often need help.

Social-networking sites are businesses and should be expected to act responsibly.

Proponents of social-networking sites love to talk about the many advantages they have for users—how they encourage friendship, civic involvement, and creativity. They forget, however, that the main reason these sites exist is so people and corporations can make money. Sites that encourage people to reveal extensive information about themselves are an advertising executive's dream come true. Based on what a person writes about himself or herself—the bands, movies, or products he or she likes or groups that he or she joins—a social-networking site can deliver advertisements to that person that are likely to be something of interest and therefore more likely to provoke a sale.

While the operators of social-networking sites have denied that they have the ability to control how people use their sites, critics reject this notion. They say that such a position amounts to the operators putting profits above the safety of the nation's children. Various ideas have been suggested as to how social-networking sites could be required to do more to put children over profits. For example, one school system technology official suggested that Congress could "require social networking sites to commit some of their prominent advertising space to public service announcements [educating parents and students about the risk of sexual predators]. That way, those who profit from these sites will bear some of those costs."[1]

Many critics, however, say that education is insufficient, and that social-networking sites need to keep younger children off their sites completely. The sites are profiting from having members who are too young to protect themselves, they say. As Dannahey observed, establishing a single standard for social-networking sites would be preferable to allowing each site to set its own rules for access by minors. Because the sites are trying to make a profit, a single site would be less willing to

implement strict standards because it might mean losing customers. Dannahey testified before Congress:

> I think what would really help [is] if the social network-
> ing sites themselves had some industry-wide standard.
> The problem always is, especially when you are dealing
> with teens, if one of the sites is doing a great job of
> enhancing their security, I think oftentimes that might
> discourage their teens who are their customers from
> being on that site so they may gravitate to a site who has
> very lax standards. So being that they are all for-profit
> companies and need members to exist or whatever, I
> think if all sites had some very similar safety standards,
> that it would kind of be an even playing field.[2]

Any risk of exposing children to sexual abuse is unacceptable.

According to research, child sexual abuse that takes place after an
online meeting consists primarily of men who *do not* lie about
their age when explicitly soliciting sex from older female adolescents. This itself leads to the criminal activity of statutory rape,
in which an adult has sex with a minor who has not reached the
age at which she can legally consent to sex. Touting such research
as an argument against restrictions on social-networking sites,
however, ignores the fact that some sexual predators *do* in fact lie
about their identity and *do* use the Internet to dupe minors into
meeting in person and then forcibly assaulting them.

When questioned as to what type of effect could be expected
from a law limiting access to social-networking sites at schools
and libraries, Bucks County, Pennsylvania, Assistant District
Attorney David Zellis said:

> It is very hard to say. If we could save one child then it
> is worth it, because that one child, that innocent child
> who may fall prey during the school hours or at a public
> school to a sexual predator because the legislation

wasn't enacted, would just be a catastrophe for that child, for that family, and for that child for the rest of his or her life.[3]

Social-networking sites should not undermine parents' and schools' efforts to protect children. Government agencies, nonprofit organizations, school systems, and even the social-networking sites themselves have developed

THE LETTER OF THE LAW

Keeping the Internet Devoid of Sexual Predators Act of 2008

Public Law No. 110-400, 110th Congress, 2nd Session (October 13, 2008)

In 2008, Congress passed a law requiring sex offenders to provide information about their online identities to state sex offender registries, although the law does not actually require social-networking sites to exclude sex offenders. The major sites have, however, agreed to do this voluntarily. The following is an excerpt from the law:

> The Attorney General ... shall require that each sex offender provide to the sex offender registry those Internet identifiers the sex offender uses or will use of any type that the Attorney General determines to be appropriate under that Act.... As used in this Act, the term "Internet identifiers" means electronic mail addresses and other designations used for self-identification or routing in Internet communication or posting....
>
> The Attorney General shall establish and maintain a secure system that permits social networking websites to compare the information contained in the National Sex Offender Registry with the Internet identifiers of users of the social networking websites, and view only those Internet identifiers that match....
>
> Nothing in this section shall be construed to require any Internet website, including a social networking website, to use the system, and no Federal or State liability, or any other actionable adverse consequence, shall be imposed on such website based on its decision not to do so.

educational materials for parents to help them keep their children safe online. An unfortunate aspect of social-networking sites, however, is that the sites make it easy for children to do unsafe things. For example, the federal government's OnGuard Online site warns parents:

> Help your kids understand what information should be private. Tell them why it's important to keep some things—about themselves, family members and friends—to themselves. Information like their full name . . . street address, [and] phone number . . . is private and should stay that way. Tell them not to choose a screen name that gives away too much personal information.[4]

Social-networking sites allow minors to post such information. Although the profiles of 14- and 15-year-olds on MySpace are supposed to be private, this requirement is easily circumvented by young people who lie about their ages. The outraged parents of a 14-year-old girl who was sexually assaulted by a 19-year-old man whom she met on MySpace unsuccessfully sued the operators of the site, with the parents' attorney arguing, "MySpace could have implemented technology . . . that would have prevented these two people from ever meeting. We wanted to keep the foxes out of the hen house."[5]

Additionally, the ease with which someone can sign up for an account, without providing any verification of identity or requiring any payment, makes it quite easy for children to create multiple profiles. OnGuard Online advises, "Review your child's friends list. You may want to limit your child's online 'friends' to people your child actually knows and is friendly with in real life."[6] When children can create multiple profiles easily, however, it makes it much more difficult for parents to monitor their children's activities.

Many parents supported the Deleting Online Predators Act, which would have blocked access to social-networking sites for minors in schools and public libraries. Even if parents monitor their children's Internet use at home, being able to access social-networking sites elsewhere creates risks. One parent pleaded, "It

THE LETTER OF THE LAW

Excerpt from the Protect Children from Sexual Predators Act, North Carolina Senate Bill 132 (February 14, 2007)

§ 14-318.5. Requiring parental permission for minors to access social networking Web sites.

(a) Definitions.—The following definitions apply in this section....

    (3) Protected computer.—Any computer that, at the time of an alleged violation of any provision of this section involving that computer, was located within the geographic boundaries of the State of North Carolina.

    (4) Social networking Web site.—A Web site on the Internet that contains profile web pages of the members of the Web site containing the name or nickname of the member, photographs placed on the profile web page by the member, and other personal information about the member; contains links to other profile web pages on the social networking Web site of friends or associates of the member that can be accessed by other members or visitors to the Web site; and provides members of or visitors to the social networking Web site the ability to leave messages or comments on the profile web page that are visible to all or some visitors to the profile web page and may also include a form of electronic mail for members of the social networking Web site.

(b) Offense.—It is unlawful for the owner or operator of a social networking Web site to allow a minor using a protected computer to become a member or to create or maintain a profile web page on a social networking Web site without the permission of the minor's parent or guardian and without providing the parent or guardian access to the profile web page at all times. The identity of the parent or guardian shall be verified by comparing the personal information provided by the parent or guardian against information found in databases containing information aggregated about individuals.

is my great hope that Congress will assist parents, like me, who are intensely concerned about our children's moral and spiritual development. It is time that Congress steps in to help parents protect their children."[7]

It is reasonable to expect social-networking sites to use all available technology to protect children.

One of the biggest controversies relating to social-networking sites is whether standards for age verification should be set in law. Traditional methods of age validation do not work well with young social-networking users. Because the sites are free, credit card verification does not work. Some sites compare information supplied by users to public records databases. Because some sites allow users who are too young to drive, however, they are not necessarily included in these databases.

In 2007, Roy Cooper, the attorney general of North Carolina, supported legislation that would have required social-networking sites to obtain parental permission before allowing any minor to access the site from a computer in North Carolina and to provide parents access to the profile. While this bill never became law, Cooper remained in the forefront of the battle against minors being allowed unfettered access to social-networking sites. In 2009, he told the *Wall Street Journal*:

> Facebook, MySpace, and other social networking sites do bear some responsibility for helping to protect kids. Clearly the main responsibility is on parents. Law enforcement must work hard to arrest predators. But because technology companies are providing this gathering space and encouraging children to come, they have a duty to put in place technology that can help protect kids.[8]

Summary

While Congress has passed a law helping social-networking sites to identify online predators, no meaningful restrictions have been placed on the way these sites operate. Frustrated parents are upset that children can easily circumvent the safeguards the sites have voluntarily put into place and want Congress to implement stronger restrictions, such as age-verification technology and banning social-networking sites from schools and libraries.

Can the Internet Be Tamed?

In order to protect the nation against the new threats of global terrorism, the Pentagon has developed its most expensive weapons program ever, including the F-35 Joint Strike Fighter. A fighter jet capable of vertical take-off and landing, it has the versatility for use in densely populated areas without runways or landing strips. Relying on millions of lines of computer code to control its movements, the jet gives the United States and its allies a huge tactical advantage.

Unfortunately, people hostile to the United States and its allies breached the project's data, downloading huge amounts of computer code that could be used to help enemies understand the operation of the F-35. According to a report by the *Wall Street Journal* in April 2009, it is thought that these "cyber-attacks" originated in China. The loss of data by the Pentagon highlights the fact that it is not only naïve children and consumers who are vulnerable to Internet crime—even the most secure military systems are vulnerable. While the incident shows how important it is to stop Internet crime, it also shows just how challenging the task is.

Regulation of the Internet is difficult because its nature is ever-changing.

On Capitol Hill, the issues that often get the most attention are the ones that have exploded in popularity before parents, teachers, and legislators really understand them. In 1998, for example, Congress passed the Digital Millennium Copyright Act (DMCA). Yet only a year into the millennium, Congress was holding hearings about teenagers and college students swapping music on Napster and other peer-to-peer services—something that legislators had never considered when they passed the Digital Millennium Copyright Act.

The DMCA created restrictions based on the technology that was available at the time. For example, the law prohibited manufacturing or importing certain VHS or Beta videocassette recorders (VCRs). The law also addressed some of the concerns that the music industry had in 1998, such as satellite radio. One provision of the law was that satellite radio providers could not publish their song lists in advance, thus enabling people to make recordings of the songs as they played. Only a few years later, virtually any song ever recorded to a CD could be downloaded without any payment using the song-swapping service Napster.

While legal challenges by record companies ultimately had Napster and similar services declared illegal under existing copyright laws, they lost revenue during a time when millions of people were freely downloading songs without paying. At the time, critics of the record companies said that they should be developing their own business model for selling music online instead of attacking Napster. In the end, it was probably a combination of the successful legal challenge and the innovation by Apple that has made the computer company's iTunes Music

Store such a huge success: It sold more than one billion song downloads in 2006, along with millions of television episodes and feature-length movies.

The key to record companies' (partial) victory over song-swapping services such as Napster and Grokster was that courts are able to interpret laws by applying new technology to existing law. The original copyright law was broad enough to prohibit distributing software that allowed easy sharing of copyrighted music. In passing subsequent laws regulating the Internet, Congress has shown the recognition that technology is ever-changing and therefore new rules will be needed. In 2008, for example, Congress amended the 2000 Children's Internet Protection Act, which requires libraries and schools to establish Internet safety policies in order to qualify for federal telecommunications funds. When Congress passed this law in 2000, social-networking sites such as MySpace did not exist, and therefore the law could not possibly mention them. When Congress passed the Protecting Children in the 21st Century Act in 2008, it required the Federal Trade Commission, a federal agency charged with consumer protection, to report to Congress each year on children's Internet safety.

Companies have invested millions in technology to make the Internet safer.

Some people say that regulation of the Internet by Congress is not the answer. There is even more opposition to regulation of the Internet by the states. Groups such as NetChoice have opposed state laws to regulate Internet auctions, social-networking sites, and online resale of sports and concert tickets. Advocates of an unrestricted Internet say that computer programmers are much more adept at responding to problems facing Internet users than are legislators. For example, states have passed laws restricting "spyware," but private vendors have been developing anti-spyware software that works more quickly and efficiently than investigations by law enforcement officers.

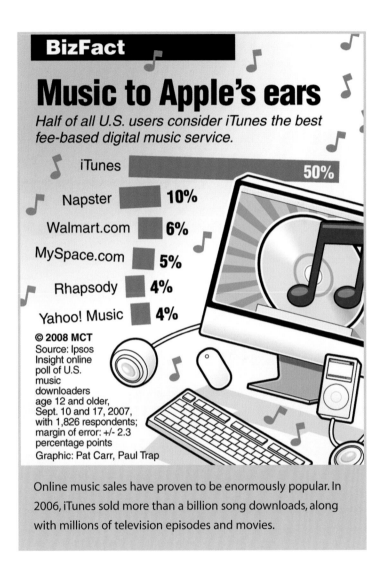

BizFact

Music to Apple's ears

Half of all U.S. users consider iTunes the best fee-based digital music service.

Service	Percent
iTunes	50%
Napster	10%
Walmart.com	6%
MySpace.com	5%
Rhapsody	4%
Yahoo! Music	4%

© 2008 MCT
Source: Ipsos Insight online poll of U.S. music downloaders age 12 and older, Sept. 10 and 17, 2007, with 1,826 respondents; margin of error: +/- 2.3 percentage points
Graphic: Pat Carr, Paul Trap

Online music sales have proven to be enormously popular. In 2006, iTunes sold more than a billion song downloads, along with millions of television episodes and movies.

At a May 2009 hearing, a congressional subcommittee examined the issue of "cybersecurity." Members of Congress had expressed concern that terrorists could disrupt the flow of traffic on the Internet. Because the nation's infrastructure has become so dependent on online communication, a major disruption of the Internet could have serious consequences, including shutting down electricity delivery systems, crippling telephone communication, and interfering with the government's ability to deliver information to the public. Greg Nojeim of the Center

Excerpt from the Georgia Computer Security Act of 2005, Ga. Code Ann. Sec. 16-9-152 (May 10, 2005)

(a) It shall be illegal for a person or entity that is not an authorized user ... of a computer in this state to knowingly, willfully, or with conscious indifference or disregard cause computer software to be copied onto such computer and use the software to do any of the following:

(1) Modify, through intentionally deceptive means, any of the following settings related to the computer's access to, or use of, the Internet:

(A) The page that appears when an authorized user launches an Internet browser or similar software program used to access and navigate the Internet;

(B) The default provider or web proxy the authorized user uses to access or search the Internet; or

(C) The authorized user's list of bookmarks used to access web pages;

(2) Collect, through intentionally deceptive means, personally identifiable information that meets any of the following criteria:

(A) It is collected through the use of a keystroke-logging function that records all keystrokes made by an authorized user who uses the computer and transfers that information from the computer to another person; [or]

(B) It includes all or substantially all of the websites visited by an authorized user, other than websites of the provider of the software, if the computer software was installed in a manner designed to conceal from all authorized users of the computer the fact that the software is being installed....

(4) Intentionally misrepresent that software will be uninstalled or disabled by an authorized user's action, with knowledge that the software will not be so uninstalled or disabled; or

(5) Through intentionally deceptive means, remove, disable, or render inoperative security, antispyware, or antivirus software installed on the computer.

for Democracy and Technology noted, however, that the private sector has been developing sophisticated systems for maintaining network security because it is in its economic self-interest: "Most critical infrastructure computer networks are maintained by the private sector. Private sector operators already monitor those systems on a routine basis to detect and respond promptly to any possible attacks, and it is often in their best business interest to continue to ramp up these defenses."[1]

With businesses and individuals already having strong motivation to maintain network security, Nojeim warned that giving the federal government control over private computer networks that are attached to the Internet was not the answer:

> CDT strongly believes that no governmental entity should be involved in monitoring private networks as part of a cybersecurity initiative. This is the job of the private sector communications service providers themselves, not of the government. Instead, the government should help develop the tools that allow providers to do this in the least intrusive way. Effective cybersecurity does not require that backbone providers give governmental entities access to the communications that flow through their networks.[2]

According to Nojeim, the risk of government involvement in cybersecurity is that such efforts could lead to censorship:

> While it is appropriate to require authentication of a user of an information system that controls the electric power grid, it would not be appropriate to require authentication of ordinary Americans surfing the Internet on their home computers. Approaches to cybersecurity that would eliminate pseudonymous and anonymous speech online would put privacy at risk, chill free expression and erode the Internet's essential openness.[3]

Additionally, giving the federal government control over private networks would give the government leverage over private businesses—a way of forcing them to do something the government wanted:

> Some have proposed that the President ought to be given authority to limit or shut down Internet traffic to a compromised critical infrastructure information system in an emergency. . . . Such power over private networks . . . would pose other risks, enabling a President to coerce costly, questionable—even illegal—conduct by threatening to shut down a system.[4]

The level of awareness of crime on the Internet is increasing.

Often, one of the driving forces behind legislation is "unsuspecting victims." As millions of people with little technical knowledge flooded onto the Internet, as well as relatively naïve young people, Internet crime had millions of potential victims. Some of the motivation to regulate online auctions, Internet pharmacies, and social networks is that the public was unaware of the potential dangers associated with the use of these applications.

Some studies, however, suggest that public awareness of Internet crime is increasing, and that as the public becomes more Internet-savvy, quick communication with the public might be more efficient than the time-consuming legislative process. For example, a 2007 study by the Pew Internet and American Life Project found that of the less than one-third of teens who had been contacted online by someone whom they had never met, two-thirds ignored or immediately deleted the contact, while about one in five asked for additional information.[5] The same study found that 85 percent of parents have rules regarding Internet use by their children, including the sites their children can visit and the type of information that they can share online. Fewer parents regulate the types of television shows their children can watch or the types of video games they play. Similarly, more parents regulate the amount of time children can spend online than regulate the amount of time that children can spend watching television or playing video games.

As technology develops, so do ways of evading it.

Of course, what is less certain is the effectiveness of the measures schools, parents, and libraries are taking to monitor children's Internet use. At the time that Congress was considering the Deleting Online Predators Act, which would have required schools and libraries to block social-networking sites such as MySpace, some school administrators complained that the measure was unnecessary and would create additional bureaucratic hassles because most schools were already blocking MySpace, Facebook, and other sites.

As quickly as schools ban a popular service such as MySpace, however, teens are finding a way around the ban. As early as 2006, the national media was reporting on how students had set up their home computers to act as a "proxy," or go-between, that allowed them to access MySpace. While MySpace was blocked, the home computer was not. Today, numerous sites exist for the specific purpose of teaching teens to get onto MySpace at school. School administrators and filtering software manufacturers have their hands full trying to keep up with these sites and blocking new techniques once they begin to circulate. Other schools have a different approach: They allow access only to "approved" sites rather than blocking unapproved sites. Who knows, however, whether the Internet really can be tamed?

Summary

Regulation of the Internet is difficult, because the problems for users are ever-changing. Problems that seemed significant just a few years ago, such as spam, have been rendered almost irrelevant by improved technology. New uses of the Internet, however, such as social networking, create new problems not covered by existing laws. While state legislatures might be able to react more quickly than the U.S. Congress, legislators seem to be trailing in a race in which network security experts and "hackers" battle for the lead.

Beginning Legal Research

The goals of each book in the POINT/COUNTERPOINT series are not only to give the reader a basic introduction to a controversial issue affecting society, but also to encourage the reader to explore the issue more fully. This Appendix is meant to serve as a guide to the reader in researching the current state of the law as well as exploring some of the public policy arguments as to why existing laws should be changed or new laws are needed.

Although some sources of law can be found primarily in law libraries, legal research has become much faster and more accessible with the advent of the Internet. This Appendix discusses some of the best starting points for free access to laws and court decisions, but surfing the Web will uncover endless additional sources of information. Before you can research the law, however, you must have a basic understanding of the American legal system.

The most important source of law in the United States is the Constitution. Originally enacted in 1787, the Constitution outlines the structure of our federal government, as well as setting limits on the types of laws that the federal government and state governments can enact. Through the centuries, a number of amendments have added to or changed the Constitution, most notably the first 10 amendments, which collectively are known as the "Bill of Rights" and which guarantee important civil liberties.

Reading the plain text of the Constitution provides little information. For example, the Constitution prohibits "unreasonable searches and seizures" by the police. To understand concepts in the Constitution, it is necessary to look to the decisions of the U.S. Supreme Court, which has the ultimate authority in interpreting the meaning of the Constitution. For example, the U.S. Supreme Court's 2001 decision in *Kyllo v. United States* held that scanning the outside of a person's house using a heat sensor to determine whether the person is growing marijuana is an unreasonable search—if it is done without first getting a search warrant from a judge. Each state also has its own constitution and a supreme court that is the ultimate authority on its meaning.

Also important are the written laws, or "statutes," passed by the U.S. Congress and the individual state legislatures. As with constitutional provisions, the U.S. Supreme Court and the state supreme courts are the ultimate authorities in interpreting the meaning of federal and state laws, respectively. However, the U.S. Supreme Court might find that a state law violates the U.S. Constitution, and a state supreme court might find that a state law violates either the state or U.S. Constitution.

Not every controversy reaches either the U.S. Supreme Court or the state supreme courts, however. Therefore, the decisions of other courts are also important. Trial courts hear evidence from both sides and make a decision, while appeals courts review the decisions made by trial courts. Sometimes rulings from appeals courts are appealed further to the U.S. Supreme Court or the state supreme courts.

Lawyers and courts refer to statutes and court decisions through a formal system of citations. Use of these citations reveals which court made the decision or which legislature passed the statute, and allows one to quickly locate the statute or court case online or in a law library. For example, the Supreme Court case *Brown v. Board of Education* has the legal citation 347 U.S. 483 (1954). At a law library, this 1954 decision can be found on page 483 of volume 347 of the U.S. Reports, which are the official collection of the Supreme Court's decisions. On the following page, you will find samples of all the major kinds of legal citation.

Finding sources of legal information on the Internet is relatively simple thanks to "portal" sites such as findlaw.com and lexisone.com, which allow the user to access a variety of constitutions, statutes, court opinions, law review articles, news articles, and other useful sources of information. For example, findlaw.com offers access to all Supreme Court decisions since 1893. Other useful sources of information include gpo.gov, which contains a complete copy of the U.S. Code, and thomas.loc.gov, which offers access to bills pending before Congress, as well as recently passed laws. Of course, the Internet changes every second of every day, so it is best to do some independent searching.

Of course, many people still do their research at law libraries, some of which are open to the public. For example, some state governments and universities offer the public access to their law collections. Law librarians can be of great assistance, as even experienced attorneys need help with legal research from time to time.

Common Citation Forms

Source of Law	Sample Citation	Notes
U.S. Supreme Court	*Employment Division v. Smith*, 485 U.S. 660 (1988)	The U.S. Reports is the official record of Supreme Court decisions. There is also an unofficial Supreme Court ("S. Ct.") reporter.
U.S. Court of Appeals	*United States v. Lambert*, 695 F.2d 536 (11th Cir.1983)	Appellate cases appear in the Federal Reporter, designated by "F." The 11th Circuit has jurisdiction in Alabama, Florida, and Georgia.
U.S. District Court	*Carillon Importers, Ltd. v. Frank Pesce Group, Inc.*, 913 F.Supp. 1559 (S.D.Fla.1996)	Federal trial-level decisions are reported in the Federal Supplement ("F. Supp."). Some states have multiple federal districts; this case originated in the Southern District of Florida.
U.S. Code	Thomas Jefferson Commemoration Commission Act, 36 U.S.C., §149 (2002)	Sometimes the popular names of legislation—names with which the public may be familiar—are included with the U.S. Code citation.
State Supreme Court	*Sterling v. Cupp*, 290 Ore. 611, 614, 625 P.2d 123, 126 (1981)	The Oregon Supreme Court decision is reported in both the state's reporter and the Pacific regional reporter.
State Statute	Pennsylvania Abortion Control Act of 1982, 18 Pa. Cons. Stat. 3203-3220 (1990)	States use many different citation formats for their statutes.

Cases and Statutes

Communications Decency Act of 1996
This federal law, struck down by the U.S. Supreme Court, would have banned transmitting "indecent" materials on the Internet.

Reno v. ACLU, 521 U.S. 884 (1997)
The U.S. Supreme Court held that the Communications Decency Act's standards for online communications violated the First Amendment to the U.S. Constitution's guarantee of free speech.

Child Online Protection Act, Public Law No. 105-277 (1998)
This federal law, struck down by the U.S. Supreme Court, would have required commercial pornography sites to deny access to minors.

Digital Millennium Copyright Act, Public Law No. 105-304 (1998)
This federal law attempted to clarify how the Internet and other electronic technologies were governed by federal copyright law but was already partially obsolete within a few years because of changes in technology.

Children's Internet Protection Act, Public Law No. 106-544 (2000)
This federal law requires schools and libraries to install blocking or filtering software on computers accessible to minors in order to receive federal financial support for Internet access.

Ashcroft v. ACLU, 535 U.S. 564 (2002)
The U.S. Supreme Court found the Child Online Protection Act, which required commercial pornography sites to limit access to adults, to be an unconstitutional violation of free speech.

CAN-SPAM Act, Public Law No. 108-187 (2003)
This federal law puts strict limits on unsolicited commercial e-mail, or "spam."

United States v. American Library Association, 539 U.S. 194 (2003)
The U.S. Supreme Court upheld the Children's Internet Protection Act, which requires libraries and schools to install blocking or filtering software if they wish to receive federal funding for electronic communication.

Metro-Goldwyn-Mayer Studios v. Grokster, 545 U.S. 913 (2005)
The U.S. Supreme Court held that the manufacturer of file-sharing software was liable for its users reproducing copyrighted music without the copyright owners' permission.

United States v. Wasz, 450 F.3d 720 (7th Cir., 2006)
A federal appeals court upheld the sentences of people convicted of selling stolen merchandise on eBay.

Doe v. MySpace, 528 F.3d 413 (5th Cir. 2008)
A federal appeals court held that MySpace could not be held liable in a case in which a minor was sexually assaulted by an adult whom she met on the social-networking site.

Protecting Children in the 21st Century Act, Public Law No. 110-382 (2008)

This federal law updated the requirements of the Children's Internet Protection Act, encouraging schools and libraries to educate children about the potential dangers of sharing information on social-networking sites.

Keeping the Internet Devoid of Sexual Predators Act, Public Law No. 110-400 (2008)

This federal law established a mechanism for social-networking sites to identify convicted sex offenders using their services, but it stopped short of requiring the sites to exclude them.

Ryan Haight Online Pharmacy Consumer Protection Act, Public Law No. 110-425 (2008)

This federal law prohibits the sale of controlled substances over the Internet unless the recipient has a valid prescription issued, in most cases, only after an in-person examination by a physician.

Terms and Concepts

Age verification

Alias

Auction

Blocking/filtering software

Controlled substance

Copyright

Cyberbullying

Cybersecurity

E-fencing

Harmful to minors

Identity theft

Indecent/obscene

Internet

Medical practice act

Online marketplace

Online prescribing

Online privacy

Organized retail crime

Prescription drug

Rogue online pharmacy

Sex offender registry

Social networking

Spam

Spyware

Statutory rape

Telemedicine

Transaction costs

Viral (video, marketing, etc.)

Introduction: Safe Surfing

1 OnGuard Online, "Email Scams," February 2008, http://www.onguardonline.gov/topics/email-scams.aspx.
2 *Reno v. ACLU*, 521 U.S. 884 (1997).
3 Child Online Protection Act, Public Law No. 105-277, 105th Cong., 2nd sess. (October 21, 1998).
4 *Ashcroft v. ACLU*, 535 U.S. 564 (2002).
5 *U.S. v. American Library Association*, 539 U.S. 194 (2003).
6 Children's Internet Protection Act, Public Law No. 106-544, 106th Cong., 2nd sess. (December 21, 2000).
7 Digital Millennium Copyright Act, Public Law No. 105-304, 105th Cong., 2nd sess. (October 28, 1998).
8 *Metro-Goldwyn-Mayer Studios v. Grokster*, 545 U.S. 913 (2005).
9 Controlling the Assault of Non-Solicited Pornography and Marketing Act, Public Law No. 108-187, 108th Cong., 1st sess. (December 16, 2003).

Point: Regulation of Online Auction and Classified Sites Will Hurt Commerce

1 EBay Stores Success Stories, "How eBay Stores Are Helping One Numismatist Get to the Top," http://pages.ebay.com/storefronts/success/aucpro.html.
2 Newark, N.J., *Star Ledger*, "Don't Do Retailers' Bidding," October 6, 2008, http://blog.nj.com/njv_editorial_page/2008/10/dont_do_retailers_bidding.html.
3 House Judiciary Committee, E-Fencing Enforcement Act of 2008, the Organized Retail Crime Act of 2008, and the Combating Organized Retail Crime Act of 2008, 110th Cong., 2nd sess., September 22, 2008, p. 23.
4 NetChoice, "Everything Old is New Again—Big Retailers Going After E-commerce Once More," February 25, 2009, http://blog.netchoice.org/2009/02/everything-old-is-new-again-big-retailers-going-after-ecommerce-again.html.
5 House Judiciary Committee, E-Fencing Enforcement Act of 2008, the Organized Retail Crime Act of 2008, and the Combating Organized Retail Crime Act of 2008, 110th Congress, 2nd Session, September 22, 2008, p. 24.

6 Ibid., p. 23.
7 *Star-Ledger*, "Don't Do Retailers' Bidding."
8 House Judiciary Committee, Organized Retail Theft Prevention: Fostering a Comprehensive Public-Private Response, 110th Cong., 1st sess., October 25, 2007, pp. 24–25.
9 House Judiciary Committee, E-Fencing Enforcement Act, p. 26.
10 Ibid.
11 Ibid.

Counterpoint: Laws Are Needed to Curb Sales of Stolen Merchandise Online

1 House Judiciary Committee, Organized Retail Theft Prevention, p. 5.
2 Ariana Eunjung Cha, "Thieves Find Exactly What They're Looking for on eBay," *Washington Post*, January 6, 2005.
3 House Judiciary Committee, E-Fencing Enforcement Act, p. 37.
4 House Judiciary Committee, E-Fencing Enforcement Act, p. 2.
5 House Judiciary Committee, Organized Retail Theft Prevention, p. 5.
6 Ibid.
7 House Judiciary Committee, E-Fencing Enforcement Act, p. 14.
8 Alexandria Sage, "Retail Crime Grows with Demand for Discounts," Reuters, February 24, 2009.
9 *United States v. Wasz*, 450 F.3d 720 (7th Cir., 2006).
10 Jack Trlica, "ORC Legislation: Addressing Loss Prevention or Competition Prevention?" *Loss Prevention*, September–October 2008, p. 22.
11 Ibid.

Point: The Benefits of Online Pharmacies Far Outweigh the Risks

1 Lynn Harris, "Dr. Pill to the Rescue," *Salon*, November 7, 2005, http://dir.salon.com/story/mwt/feature/2005/11/07/e_c/index.html.
2 Oliver Ryan, "The Right Rx?" *Fortune*, March 6, 2006, http://money.cnn.com/magazines/fortune/fortune_archive/2006/03/06/8370612/index.htm.
3 House Committee on the Judiciary, Online Pharmacies and the Problem of

Internet Drug Abuse, 110th Cong., 2nd sess. (June 24, 2008), pp. 58–59.

4 Ibid.

5 Ryan Haight Act, S. 399, 109th Cong., 1st sess. (October 15, 2008).

6 House Committee on the Judiciary, Online Pharmacies, p. 57.

7 *Missouri Board of the Healing Arts v. Thompson*, No. 02-0505 HA, (Mo. Admin. Hrg. Comm'n, June 9, 2004).

8 Ibid.

9 Ibid.

10 Virginia Postrel, "Putting the Hex on Rx," *Forbes ASAP*, May 29, 2000, http://www.forbes.com/asap/2000/0529/062_print.html.

11 Ibid.

12 Mark A. Munger, Gregory J. Stoddard, Allen R. Wenner, et al., "Safety of Prescribing PDE-5 Inhibitors via e-Medicine vs. Traditional Medicine," *Mayo Clinic Proceedings* 83, No. 8 (2008), p. 894.

13 Postrel, "Putting the Hex on Rx."

14 Munger, et al., "Safety of Prescribing PDE-5 Inhibitors via e-Medicine vs. Traditional Medicine," p. 895.

15 Bob Tedeschi, "Pharmacies Endorse Crackdown on Fraud," *New York Times*, October 24, 2005, http://www.nytimes.com/2005/10/24/technology/24ecom.html.

16 House Committee on the Judiciary, Online Pharmacies, p. 56.

17 U.S. Government Accountability Office, "Internet Pharmacies: Some Pose Risks for Consumers," GAO 04-820 (June 2004), p. 6.

Counterpoint: Public Safety Demands Stronger Regulation of Online Pharmacies

1 Senate Committee on the Judiciary, Rogue Online Pharmacies: The Growing Problem of Internet Drug Trafficking, 110th Cong., 1st sess. (May 16, 2007), p. 6.

2 Order Granting Motion for Summary Judgment, *McKay v. Hageseth*, No. C-06-1377 MMC (N.D. Minn., September 7, 2007).

3 See http://www.christianhageseth.com.

4 Barry Yeoman, "Drugs Online: A New Danger," *Ladies' Home Journal*, May 2001, http://www.lhj.com/relationships/family/safety/drugs-online-a-new-danger/?page=1.

5 Medical Board of California, "Internet Prescribing—Information for Consumers." http://www.medbd.ca.gov/consumer/internet_prescribing.html.

6 Ibid.

7 House Committee on the Judiciary, Online Pharmacies, p. 8.

8 Senate Committee on the Judiciary, Rogue Online Pharmacies, p. 111.

9 House Committee on the Judiciary, Online Pharmacies, p. 72.

Point: Restrictions on Social Networking Will Hamper a Valuable Communications Tool

1 Ellen McGirt, "How Chris Hughes Helped Launch Facebook and the Barack Obama Campaign," *Fast Company*, April 2009, http://www.fastcompany.com/magazine/134/boy-wonder.html.

2 Jennifer Steinhauer, "Verdict in MySpace Suicide Case," *New York Times*, November 26, 2008, http://www.nytimes.com/2008/11/27/us/27myspace.html.

3 House Committee on Oversight and Government Reform, Darfur and the Olympics: A Call for International Action, 110th Congress, 1st Session (June 7, 2007), p. 21.

4 JessicaAlana31, "MySpace Is Safe and Beneficial for Teens/MySpace Pros," JessicaAlana31's Blog, September 26, 2007, http://www.progressiveu.org/195111-myspace-is-safe-and-benificial-for-teens-myspace-pros.

5 House Committee on Energy and Commerce, Sexual Exploitation of Children Over the Internet: What Parents, Kids and Congress Need To Know about Child Predators, 109th Congress, 2nd Session (April 4-May 3, 2006), p. 82.

6 American Library Association, Press Release, "ALA Disappointed by House Passage of Bill that Will Block Key Web Applications," July 26, 2006, http://www.ala.org/ala/newspresscenter/news/

pressreleases2006/july2006/dopapasses-
house.cfm.

7 Janis Wolak, David Finkelhor, and
Kimberly Mitchell, Fact Sheet, "1 in
7 Youth: The Statistics about Online
Sexual Solicitations," December 2007,
http://www.unh.edu/ccrc/internet-
crimes/1in7Youth7-09-08.pdf.

8 Michelle L. Ybarra and Kimberly J.
Mitchell, "How Risky Are Social Networking Sites? A Comparison of Places
Online Where Youth Sexual Solicitation
and Harassment Occurs," *Pediatrics*, February 2008, p. 355.

9 Keeping the Internet Devoid of Sexual
Predators (KIDS) Act, Public Law No.
110-400, 110th Congress, 2nd session
(Oct. 13, 2008).

10 Internet Safety Task Force, Harvard
Law School, *Enhancing Child Safety and
Online Technologies: Final Report of the
Internet Safety Technical Task Force to
the Multi-State Working Group on Social
Networking of State Attorneys General
of the United States*, Cambridge, Mass.:
Harvard University, 2008, p. 16.

11 Ibid.

12 Ibid.

13 Public Law No. 106-544, 106th Congress,
2nd Session (Dec. 21, 2000).

14 Public Law No. 110–385, 110th Congress, 2nd Session (Oct. 10, 2008).

15 Ibid.

16 Janice Wolak, David Finkelhor, Kim-
berly J. Mitchell, and Michele L. Ybarra,
"Online 'Predators' and Their Victims:
Myths, Realities, and Implications for
Prevention and Treatment," *American
Psychologist*, Vol. 63, No. 2, 111-128, p.
123.

17 Ibid.

18 House Committee on Energy and
Commerce, Making the Internet Safe
for Kids: The Role of ISP's and Social
Networking Sites, 109th Congress, 2nd
Session (June 27-28, 2006), p. 213.

19 Ibid., p. 216.

20 Ibid., p. 217.

21 Ibid.

**Counterpoint: Social Networks Are
Accessible to Youths and Therefore
Must Be Made Safe**

1 House Committee on Energy and Commerce, H.R. 5319, The Deleting Online
Predators Act of 2006, 109th Congress,
2nd Session (July 11, 2006), pp. 94-95.

2 House Committee, Making the Internet
Safe for Kids, p. 199.

3 House Committee on Energy and Commerce, H.R. 5319, The Deleting Online
Predators Act of 2006, 109th Congress,
2nd Session (July 11, 2006), p. 137.

4 OnGuard Online, "Social Networking
Sites," http://www.onguardonline.gov/
topics/social-networking-sites.aspx.

5 *Doe v. MySpace*, 528 F.3d 413 (5th Cir.
2008).

6 OnGuard Online, "Social Networking
Sites."

7 House Committee, The Deleting Online
Predators Act, p. 154.

8 Emily Steel, "The Case for Age
Verification," *Wall Street Journal*,
January 13, 2009, http://blogs.wsj.
com/digits/2009/01/13/the-case-for-age-
verification/tab/print/.

**Conclusion: Can the Internet Be
Tamed?**

1 House Committee on Energy and
Commerce, Cybersecurity: Network
Threats and Policy Challenges, 111th
Congress, 1st Session (May 1, 2009),
http://energycommerce.house.gov/Press_
111/20090501/testimony_nojeim.pdf.

2 Ibid.

3 Ibid.

4 Ibid.

5 Amanda Lenhart and Mary Madden,
*Teens, Privacy & Online Social Networks:
How Teens Manage Their Online Identi-
ties and Personal Information in the Age
of MySpace*, Washington, D.C.: Pew
Research Center, 2007.

RESOURCES ||||| ▷

Books and Reports

Internet Safety Task Force, Harvard Law School. *Enhancing Child Safety and Online Technologies: Final Report of the Internet Safety Technical Task Force to the Multi-State Working Group on Social Networking of State Attorneys General of the United States.* Cambridge, Mass.: Harvard University Press, 2008.

Lenhart, Amanda, and Mary Madden. *Teens, Privacy & Online Social Networks: How Teens Manage Their Online Identities and Personal Information in the Age of MySpace.* Washington, D.C.: Pew Research Center, 2007.

Web Sites

American Library Association (ALA)
http://www.ala.org
This national group representing librarians generally opposes censorship, including the requirement to install filtering software on library computers in order to receive federal Internet funding.

Center for Democracy and Technology
http://www.cdt.org
This organization generally opposes regulation of the Internet, with a special emphasis on making the Internet available to all and protecting free speech.

Crimes Against Children Research Center, University of New Hampshire
http://www.unh.edu/ccrc/
Researchers at the center have studied the problem of online sexual solicitations (and actual abuse) indepth and believe that much of the rhetoric regarding protection of youths is exaggerated or inaccurate.

Electronic Frontier Foundation
http://www.eff.org
This organization opposes government surveillance of and interference with Internet use and supports loose interpretation of copyright laws.

Food and Drug Administration (FDA)
http://www.fda.gov
The federal agency that regulates prescription drugs offers guidance on the safety of online prescribing.

National Clearinghouse on Internet Prescribing, Federation of State Medical Boards
http://www.fsmb.org/ncip_overview.html
The Federation of State Medical Boards, which opposes writing prescriptions without an in-patient examination, maintains information on physicians who

112

have been disciplined by a state so that other states' medical boards are aware of the result.

National Retail Federation

http://www.nrf.com

This association of retail chains supports legislation that would make it more difficult to sell stolen property in online marketplaces.

NetChoice

http://www.netchoice.org

This association of online sellers opposes stricter regulation of the Internet.

OnGuard Online

http://www.onguardonline.gov

The federal government maintains up-to-date information about self-protection from Internet crime.

Operation Cyber Sweep

http://www.fbi.gov/cyber/cysweep/cysweep1.htm

The Federal Bureau of Investigation offers information about its ongoing efforts to stop Internet-based crime.

Pew Internet and American Life Project

http://www.pewinternet.org

The research arm of the charitable foundation conducts extensive research through surveys and focus groups and makes available detailed information about Americans' use of the Internet.

Verified Internet Pharmacy Practice Sites, National Association of Boards of Pharmacy

http://www.nabp.net/indexvipps.asp

The National Association of Boards of Pharmacy maintains a list of pharmacies that abide by good practices such as selling only drugs approved for U.S. sale and requiring a legitimate prescription.

PICTURE CREDITS

ALAN MARZILLI, M.A., J.D., lives in Birmingham, Ala., and is a program associate with Advocates for Human Potential, Inc., a research and consulting firm based in Sudbury, Mass., and Albany, N.Y. He works primarily on developing training and educational materials for agencies of the federal government on topics such as housing, mental health policy, employment, and transportation. He has spoken on mental health issues in 30 states, the District of Columbia, and Puerto Rico; his work has included training mental health administrators, nonprofit management and staff, and people with mental illnesses and their families on a wide variety of topics, including effective advocacy, community-based mental health services, and housing. He has written several handbooks and training curricula that are used nationally and as far away as the territory of Guam. He managed statewide and national mental health advocacy programs and worked for several public interest lobbying organizations while studying law at Georgetown University. He has written more than a dozen books, including numerous titles in the POINT/COUNTERPOINT series.